Love and Peanut Butter

LESLEY CONGER

This is the light-hearted celebration of an ordinary year in the Conger household, with the seasons marked off as a mother sees them – by tinsel and muddy galoshes, the green shreds of an Easter bunny's nest, soggy swimsuits and sandy beach towels, and a gummy bag of Halloween treats – and by *Love and Peanut Butter* all year round. There are eight Congers – two little girls, four medium-sized boys, and two grown-ups. They are the family that lives in the big old house down the street; that's one of their sons who just delivered the paper, and that lady pushing around a loaded grocery cart with a shopping list clutched in her teeth is Mrs. Conger.

She is quite a woman, even though her children call her "the meanest mother on the block." She has written a warm and delightful chronicle of her family's ups and down, interspersed with her own pungent comments on

[*Continued on back flap*]

LESLEY CONGER

LOVE AND PEANUT BUTTER

Drawings by DOUG ANDERSON

NEW YORK

W · W · NORTON & COMPANY · INC ·

First Edition

Acknowledgment is made to the Canadian Broadcasting Corporation for material which was originally written for radio broadcast and has been included here in revised form.

Library of Congress Catalog Card No. 61-7475

Printed in the United States of America
for the Publishers by the Vail-Ballou Press
1 2 3 4 5 6 7 8 9

To

H. L.

LOVE AND PEANUT BUTTER

"IT WOULD be more interesting," my husband said, "if somebody sent us all to New Guinea. You could write a book about that."

But my husband is an anthropologist and has ulterior motives; the natives always look browner in somebody else's back yard.

"No, that isn't what I want to do."

"You mean you want to write about a year that nothing happened in?"

"Mm-hm. That's the kind of year most years are, anyway. Suppose we went to New Guinea and then wrote about it—why, all the rest of our lives we'd be Those People Who Went to New Guinea. It'd be a gross misrepresentation. The truth is, we spend most of our lives *not* going to New Guinea. Most people do."

"Just an ordinary year, then?"

"A plain, ordinary year. It's the kind of year I know the most about."

"I suppose so."

I had to make some kind of concession. "We could go to New Guinea some other time. Later on."

"Well, when I said New Guinea I didn't really mean New Guinea anyway. I just happened to say New Guinea." And he was, I knew, scanning on the screen of his mind a map he carries with him (along with sharp memories of childhood and a shaky grasp of the multiplication table) showing all the islands of the world, very green against the very blue waters.

"A plain, ordinary year, January through December." I pulled the blankets up to my chin and spread my toes apart thoughtfully. "January," I said, thinking of New Year's Day and of brave, impossible lists of resolutions (*Which child resolved last year to dry dishes two nights a week?*). January . . .

JANUARY

JANUARY is an ambitious month, full of hope. I like it because it's a beginning and I've always liked beginnings. One of the first things we learned in high school German was a proverb, *Aller Anfang ist schwer*, and if I've got it wrong after only twenty-one years, Miss Fischer will just have to forgive me. Anyway, it means "every beginning is difficult" and it's dead wrong. In fact I might say that I am a living refutation of that proverb. Beginnings are easy; it's endings that are difficult. I've begun dozens of things—begun to read the Great Books, begun to clean the house thoroughly, begun to reduce, begun to learn to speak Russian. Nothing was easier than beginning to learn to speak Russian. Anybody can do it. But somewhere along the way I get hung up, on the third thick book or the second dirty floor or the night of the first hungry day or the declension of numerals, and I never do finish.

I just hope this book turns out to be an exception.

We always take our tree down on New Year's Eve, and since we always put it up on Christmas Eve, this makes us the last family in the neighborhood to put a tree up and the first to take it down. We've been battling the children on this score for years, while the tree lights go on in window after window up and down the street. *They* would have us putting it up earlier and earlier until, I suppose, it would be the first thing we'd do after finally persuading them to throw out the Halloween jack-o'-lantern with the top of his skull hung with long green and gray mold and his face caved in with a puckering, toothless, centenarian smile. But we've held out, even against charges of being the meanest parents in town.

Of course a dry Christmas tree *is* a fire hazard. But if you take a look at our garage with the car parked in front of it because we can't get it inside, you'll know we aren't really concerned with such a practical reason. The truth is that I can't bear to get up in the morning and start a new year with last year's tree standing there in the living room in a shaft of pale, wintry sun, looking like somebody who just got home from an all-night party—disheveled, exhausted, footsore, and slightly hung over. It isn't that we don't like Christmas trees; we just don't want to be tired of ours before we take it down.

So we put the tree up on Christmas Eve. Every other year or so another child is old enough to join the ritual, another child emancipated and wise with the knowledge that Santa Claus is really Mommy and Daddy and everybody who loves you—and wishing, wistfully, that he weren't, or at least that enlightenment could have been put off just one more year. (But, as childhood's traumatic experiences go, this may not be so much worse than finding out that the plastic model submarine that looks about a foot long on the outside of the cereal package is really the size of the first two joints of your little finger; and it may be that even a six-year-old child can perceive, in his heart if not in his head, what lies behind each of the two deceptions.) As for the tree, it is always a Douglas fir, *Pseudotsuga taxifolia,* no exceptions allowed; always as big as possible; and always green. I vaguely recall from years ago a season of aberration, probably adolescent, when I was convinced we ought to have a silver tree with blue ornaments only, but my mother must have prevailed; she could still remember the huge *Weihnachtsbaum* her father and older brothers would drag into the big room of the combination saloon-and-inn the family owned. It was enormous to begin with, but if it were not plump or symmetrical enough to suit them, they would even graft in additional branches to fill it out to perfection. What miserable spindly evergreen sprayed with a silver disguise and hung with ice-cold blue could compete with the memory of such a tree, reaching to the ceiling, smelling of the forest, and quivering with the splendid, dangerous light of candles?

We put our tree up with tremendous seriousness, moving the colored lights from socket to socket and standing back to squint at the effect, worrying about too many reds on one side and too many greens on the other. We hang the balls, lifting each one tenderly from its tissue-paper nest. Some are new, some are older than our oldest child, but there is one neither gold nor silver nor any of the shiny, gaudy colors. It is a satin white with soft green leaves and a velvet peach, and this one I remember from my own childhood and I hang it myself, trembling each year for fear it might fall and break and my heart with it. Then there are little birds to clip on the branches, and a tiny wooden angel, and candy canes, and in years when I am ambitious, decorated cookies with loops of thread to hang them by, and strings of popcorn and cranberries.

The last thing to go on the tree is the silver rain. I know it says *icicles* on the package, but I have lived most of my life in this immoderately moderate northwest climate, and to me it always looks like rain. We hang the rain patiently, precisely, strand by strand, and anyone who starts to take it heedlessly by the handful and throw it at the tree (a degraded practice followed in some savage quarters) is immediately apprehended with cries of horror and revulsion. But at last the sheet is spread beneath the tree and one of the boys crouches there in readiness, holding the light-plug while the rest of us switch off the lamps. A prickly moment of darkness—and we all sigh in unison our skyrocket-bursting, Christmas-tree-lighting-up sigh: "Aaaahhhhh!"

All that for a single week of glory and then January waits on the other side of midnight. We wrap the balls back in their tissue paper, try to save the best of the silver rain, arbitrate a fight over the one cooky somebody discovers deep in the middle of the tree, unwind the lights from the branches, and take the tree outside—where it lies around in the yard until the middle of February or maybe even March.

But all the rest of January I find fir needles in the corners of the room, under the furniture, between the rug and its mat. Occasionally a strand of silver rain, crumpled and flattened, gleams up at me from some unlikely place—upstairs under the crib, or in the kitchen behind the refrigerator. It takes a long time before it's all gone, and some years I just barely make it a few days before the place fills up with broken bits of colored eggshell and shreds of green and yellow nests. These things sadden me, the crushed tinsel and yellow, brittle fir needles, evidences of the ephemeral nature of man's joys, of the inexorable passage of time—and of the incredible sloppiness of my housekeeping.

I used to think that the New Year ought to begin on the first day of spring, so that all the new beginnings would come together: the bravest new flowers spiking from the brown earth, the haze of green shimmering down over the barren woods, the release in the heart that comes with the end of winter, and the tantalizing promise of that new number in the counting of our years. But the New Year comes, after all, when we really need it most, in the middle of the darkness of winter, which would be unbearable without it. It makes the spring move closer to have the year change in midwinter, and it is in its own way a sort of spring, a hidden, secret spring of true beginnings. The green shoots that will break through later are preparing now beneath the hard, crusty soil. The trees sleep and dream of waking; everything waits.

Inside the house there is a difference. It's still winter and will be winter for a long while, but now we're used to the boots in the hallway in their puddles of muddy water and to the smell of wet, warm wool. It's begun to grow lighter already; I notice it when the alarm shrieks at seven—now I can almost find the clock to turn it off before I dislocate my shoulder. The house itself looks different. I begin to notice things I haven't been seeing, mostly things that are dirty and things that are wearing out. In the girls' bedroom the gray kittens on the yellow curtains have faded away until from the doorway I can see only their little blue eyes gazing wistfully back at me, two and two and two. I think about a big top-to-bottom housecleaning and I buy all kinds of new and fascinating cleaning products from the Fuller Brush Man—waxes for the front hall (where the previous family, with only two children, installed elegant black and white tiling), bottles of polish and cleaner with dust-repelling silicone, everything I need except the will power to do it with.

Oh, but this will be a better year; I will do more than I have done before. Maybe this will even be the year my broken desk drawer will get repaired, or it may be the year I manage to buy a new typewriter. As the earth fills up with growing things ready to emerge, I fill up with plans and lists and promises, and I too am waiting.

My New Year's Resolutions comprise only one of the lists I make at this time of year. I am a great, indefatigable list-maker. As a maker of lists, in fact, I bow to no one, not even to my mother-in-law, who used to rise every morning and make such a long and extensive list of the things she had to do that by the time the list was complete the morning had half fled and she was too exhausted to do more than totter to the stove and pour yet another cup of coffee before lying down for a nap. I think she has recently modified this practice somewhat, but I suspect that, like myself, she is never happier and in more exuberant spirits than when making a list.

I have lists for everything. Bills to pay, chores to do, people to write, birthdays to remember, garden tools to return—these are the mundane lists I make every few days. But I have other lists—lists of things I want to buy, for example, ranging from something I might conceivably squeeze out of the household money next week to something I might conceivably get my hands on if the Aga Khan sent me a bushel of diamonds as a small token of his esteem. I have lists of things I should write and things

I should read. I have lists of self-improvement projects for everything from my figure (*Lose ten pounds*) to my disposition (*Don't yell at the kids*).

My writing notebooks, instead of being the wise, discursive, perceptive volumes that pose as writers' notebooks in the public library (I am not deceived, you fakers), are mainly lists—lists of ideas, lists of plots, lists of things I might revise, lists of things I might adapt for radio or television, lists of things I might possibly hope to sell in the next couple of months, and most of all, lists which embody elaborate schedules for getting superhuman amounts of work done, like "Work 3 hrs daily on book, 1 hr on other scripts, 2 hrs reading"—this to be sandwiched in somehow or other between washing, cooking, and cleaning for a family of nine. Such lists almost always culminate in an exquisitely worked-out chart which proves beyond all doubt that if I just sit down and write 2,000 words a day I'll have my book finished in 30 days.

Anyway, it stands to reason I am especially fond of New Year's. What other time affords such a wonderful opportunity to make really earth-shaking lists? I can toss off a dozen or more resolutions in no time at all. *Read fewer book reviews and more books. Don't write so many letters, write more stories instead. Make those curtains. Lose ten pounds.* (I write that one everywhere—it's a wonder I don't put it on my grocery lists, where, come to think of it, it might do some good.)

My husband, viewing my list-making passion with the analytical curiosity an anthropologist bends upon human foibles, long ago concluded that for me listing is a kind of magic. It really has nothing to do with jotting things down in order not to forget them; I'm not likely to forget that I need to lose ten pounds, not with my closet jammed with undersized clothes I'm longing to be able to wear, including a pretty skirt our foster daughter made one size too small and presented to me with more hope than common sense. No, I'm sure my husband is right. I write lists because I feel, in some primitive corner of my being, that if I get things on paper I have them in my power. Something listed is as good as half done. And I have more half-done lists than any other housewife in captivity, believe me.

Once a list is written, there is a rare and strange joy in crossing it out. I used to keep my general household list on the side of the refrigerator, using purple crayon; there is a marvelous, unrivaled satisfaction in crossing things out with purple crayon. The list always began with a single command: DEFROST! and as far as I can remember I've never gotten to the bottom of one of those lists before having to put DEFROST! back up on the top again. I've always felt a little sorry that we moved the refrigerator partly out of sight and I've had to go back to paper and pencil.

I've learned a lot about lists in the years I've been using them, which is quite a number of years. (I recently found an old list of mine—resolutions—dated about 1933, I think it was, inscribed blotchily on the flyleaf of a diary and beginning with *Don't bite my fingernails!* I seized a pencil and was just about to cross it out when my conscience rose up and reminded me that I still, on occasion, nip off a ragged cuticle with my teeth.) Anyway I've learned to handle lists so they don't get the better of me. A new, pristine list without any cancellations is mere vanity and empty promises, of course; and a list with everything canceled except that one thing you know you will never do (like *Lose ten pounds*) is an abomination. A list is really at its peak when it is still neat, looks ambitious, but testifies to the good intentions of its author with a moderately high percentage of firm, vigorous crossings-out. The real criterion of listmanship is the ability to keep all your lists at this peak stage.

One good approach which leads to rapid and effective crossing-out and a consequent feeling of accomplishment and virtue is list-packing. It's very simple. What you do is to be sure to put on each list a few things you want to do not because they must be done for reasons of sanitation, economy, human relations, or health (like *Lose ten pounds*)—no, things you simply *want* to do, like *Try new lpstk shade* or *Phone Irene* or *Spnd brthdy check* (before it disappears into the household money and is never seen again).

This gambit will get you off to a quick start; but toward the end you are always faced with the nasty problem of the almost-finished list that threatens to hang on forever. The solution for this is a touch of slovenliness, which to some of us comes naturally anyway. When you see that a list is reaching that never-never point, doodle on it absent-mindedly, spill nail polish on it, let the baby get near it with a color crayon or a can of strained prunes. Then you simply start a new list, copy the uncanceled items onto it, and destroy the old one—making sure, of course, to put a lot of new items on the new list so that you will have something to cross out. In this way you are never annoyed by the one or two stubborn items that survive all your best intentions. Why, I have some such items that have traveled from list to list for weeks, months, even years, each time reappearing fresh and new as if I had just conceived of doing them. Like, for example, *Lose ten pounds*.

With practice and perseverance and a little ingenuity, you see, you can develop your skill with lists to the point where you can accomplish an awful lot without doing much of anything. (My husband says he has caught me putting at the top of a list something I have already done, in order to be able to cross it out, but I haven't done that more than once or twice, or maybe three times. Or four. After all, that wouldn't really be *honest*, would it?)

So in January I make lists. I get a new notebook for my writing notes and start it off with an agenda that would take the full time of Ernest Hemingway, Georges Simenon, and a roomful of secretaries pounding typewriters eight hours a day. I ramble through the house with paper and pencil and write down everything that needs to be repaired, replaced, or given a coat of paint. I sift all the Christmas cards and make a list of all the people who enclosed letters or notes lengthy enough to qualify for an answer. And with glorious enthusiasm I buy a new stenographer's notebook and work out a careful budget for January and a slightly rougher (but no less optimistic) budget for the entire year. Even with optimism there is always a gap between the amount of our regular income and the amount we obviously need in order to survive, and that gap is mine to close, by my wits and my typewriter and through the cleverness of my agent and the softheadedness of editors and producers. It's really four gaps, one for each season: Spring, income taxes; Summer, property taxes; Fall, school clothes; Winter, Christmas. These are the four expectable financial crises of the year—never mind the ones we *can't* expect—and not one of them is small enough to be wedged into the confines of a budget.

But I love budgeting. I regard it as a challenge from some implacable, practically supernatural enemy who can never be defeated entirely. Victory lies in keeping *him* from defeating *me* entirely, and that's victory enough for anyone who can remember hamburger patties for Thanksgiving dinner back in the dear dark days of the Great Depression.

My methods of budgeting and household finance, however, would probably not appeal to an expert on home economics. I am a woman of infinitesimal economies and large extravagances. I will spend 15 minutes re-inking an old typewriter ribbon and then figure that that gives me the right to buy a $100 coat. I have cut the family hair for over a dozen years and always buy oleomargarine, but we had an encyclopedia and four kids before we had a washing machine, and I'd rather get a long-playing record of a symphony than replace a broken casserole.

You may regard this as a fault. I don't. It's a philosophy.

I just prefer life this way. I prefer a new book to a new broom, and I may not have a pair of warm gloves but I do have a new cream brocade cocktail gown. The trap under the upstairs bathroom washbasin leaks, but we have a lovely Italian glass pitcher for the living-room mantel. We use reconstituted milk for cocoa and cooking, but we eat T-bone steaks. There are some insufficiencies and economies I can tolerate and others I can't. I have never minded the fact that the one saucepan I have that doesn't stick is also the one with the handle broken off. I can go on using it for years. I wouldn't give up one of our magazine subscriptions for a whole set of cookware.

Even the things that bother me somehow get ignored and put off. An automatic washer and a dryer have been on my list of things to buy for several years now. But every time we get enough money we use it for something else. Last year we drove to Mexico and back, and ripped out the furnace and put in a new one. So I go on shoving and pulling the old wringer-washer back and forth from the kitchen sink, and I go on wiping up the oil that is slowly dripping out of the transmission, and I go on hanging the laundry on our clothesline, which is nicely situated on the north side of the house in the shade of our big old dogwood tree. If I get two good days in a row the laundry might even get dry enough to bring in, because the sun hits the last seven feet of the line at least 45 minutes a day. When it rains I hang the clothes on a rack that is suspended like the sword of Damocles above our heads in the kitchen where we eat all our meals, and it seems to be raining every weekend. But if I save carefully the next few months I think I can squeeze out enough money to have a washer and drier installed—provided we forget about that summer camp we've been wanting to send the boys to.

One writer I heard of (also a woman) spent most of her literary earnings on musical instruments for her family. They got a grand piano out of one series of checks, violins out of another. She figures maybe next year they'll get indoor plumbing.

There are nine of us, not including the animals. There weren't always nine of us, but children have a way of accumulating like yesterday's newspapers, only you can't put them in the chimney seat or tie them with twine and give them to the Salvation Army. Everybody knows, of course, that no college professor should have more than two children, a boy who can grow up to mow the lawn while Dad finishes grading 150 term essays and a girl who can wash dishes while Mom tries to convert a seven-year-old dress into something she can wear to the reception for retiring members of the staff. Any more than two are superfluous and insupportable, literally. We have six—seven if you count Virginia, but she came nearly full-grown and hasn't cost us anything but a little bit of patience with rock-and-roll, hair in the washbasin, and the ringing of the telephone.

We didn't intend to have six. People often ask us this —very tactfully of course and in a variety of ways that certainly attest to the versatility of the English language— but it all amounts to the same thing when you boil it down. I try to be as airy and nonchalant about it as possible under the circumstances. I can't really remember intending *anything*, but if I did it was to be a famous writer by the time I was twenty. I don't recall counting up either future children or future husbands, except in that fortunetelling game we kids played by picking the leaves of plantain weeds so that the number of little strands sticking out from the broken end foretold the number of children or husbands, whichever way you were playing it, we were supposed to have. But by the time I was nineteen I had one husband (the same one I have yet) and my fame as a writer was limited rather sharply to the subdued appreciation of the English teachers at Lincoln High School.

Let's not pretend. I remember my doctor telling me on the occasion of my last pregnancy, "You need this baby like you need a hole in the head." (He has a good, snappy bedside manner, rather bracing and astringent.) I left his office clutching a little bottle of Gravol pills for fighting off that morning-on-shipboard feeling. I'd never had it like this before, and he was so right: I knew I needed this baby like I needed a hole in the head. But a peculiar, unreasonable thrill kept creeping up through the nausea, and when the baby finally arrived I was transported with joy as if this were something that had never happened to me before. I suspect that if it were to happen again (and I am, for these purposes, a *mere* 36¾ years old), I'd be just as miserably sick and just as imbecilically happy. This disintegration of the logical faculty is known as Motherhood, and I wonder if my stomach isn't smarter than the rest of me?

Even the children are positive that we could do a lot more for each of them if there hadn't been so many of them. It was just the other night that Duncan, the oldest, started holding forth on this theme. If we had just one or two children (one of them would be *him,* of course) we could give them so much more individual attention, buy them better clothes and more toys, have a nicer house. . . . All of them sat silently brooding over the things each could have had had he been the only one. It was a sad moment. Then Malcolm glanced at the clock and said he was going up to take his bath. Jill, who always bathes with sister Polly, suddenly decided she wanted to have *her* bath too, so Mac magnanimously allowed she could join him. This announcement caused the sudden rending of the air with sobs and howls. *"But I'll be lonely!"* wailed Polly, envisaging the vast whiteness of the bathtub with only her small blonde self in it. These were the children who wanted to be *only* children?

It was a little crowded, but they bathed three-in-a-tub.

So there are nine of us: Wayne, who wears a beard and teaches anthropology; Virginia, who is nearly twenty and almost a chapter by herself; Duncan, who is thirteen; and downward, in this order, Andy, Malcolm, Cameron, Polly, and Jill, who is three and a half, has red hair and freckles, and was needed like a hole in the head. Last, myself, 36¾ years old at this writing, indifferent housewife, part-time writer, night-school instructor, and M-O-T-H-E-R, who needs to lose ten pounds and probably never will.

I suppose this book needs some explanation. I've often thought how the general public (those few remaining people who are not writing their own books) is deceived by the appearance of a new book on the market. Ahha, says the reader, Seymour Glutch has written a new book about a middle-aged woman who falls in love with a fifteen-year-old male pearl diver and goes back to Iowa a sadder but wiser woman. And the reader imagines Seymour, with the master plan of this novel in mind, sitting down every night to do a few more pages as chapter after chapter piles up at his elbow. The truth is probably that Seymour didn't sit down to write this book at all; he had another book in mind entirely. In fact, there is probably a book Seymour has been writing for about six years now, and this new one is only something he has written in desperation because he can't finish the book he is really writing. Behind every Glutch volume that appears there stands another, That Other, which remains steadfastly and obstinately unwritten.

This doesn't happen just to Seymour Glutch. Let's take an example near at hand: me. I have nine partly written book-length manuscripts piled up around here right now, and there is one of them I think of, constantly, as The Book I Am Supposed to Be Writing. It has been The Book I Am Supposed to Be Writing for years.

And it doesn't happen just to me and Seymour Glutch, either. Every despondent writer ought to read, without fail, Chapter 53 of *The Autobiography of Mark Twain,* wherein he discusses his own literary shipyard strewn with the hulls of half-finished ships. (This is heartening, like discovering that Thomas Edison was considered a dull boy in school or like pondering, in moments of despair, the fact that even William Shakespeare must have had a wastebasket.)

Meanwhile, in his literary shipyard, the writer bangs together a dinghy or two, or maybe a barely floatable raft, just to keep body and soul together and to convince himself that he can build and has every good intention of building seaworthy vessels. Me, I've been whacking this dinghy together for years, in letters to friends and family, in radio talks over the Canadian Broadcasting Corporation network, and in mumbling conversation with myself (as the only available adult listener) as I feed blue jeans through the wringer or beat up a seven-minute icing. It's about time I sat down and wrote it for real, so I can get it out of my system.

You mustn't think of me, incidentally, as sitting down each evening in a quiet corner of the house (where?) to pen, thoughtfully, a few more pages of this manuscript. By night I am not fit to write a book; I am barely fit to write the next day's shopping list. This book is being written in bits and pieces, interrupted by letting the dog in and out, finding lost mittens and a Grade Seven math book, and wrestling a small child in and out of a snowsuit and boots.

(Did you know that there is an immutable law that says that a small child will have to go to the toilet exactly 1 min. 27 sec. after being zipped into a snowsuit and let out the front door, 3 min. 38 sec. after being tucked into bed, 5 min. 43 sec. after boarding a bus; and that a boy of ten will have to go the toilet 10 min. 05 sec. after the feature movie starts in a theater and at 15-minute intervals thereafter?)

I've read a number of books that celebrate the passage of the seasons in the country or in the wilderness, with the annual round of crops, the flight of geese, the yearly appearance of various animals and plants, the cycle of the weather. But the year passes for us on a city street, the seasons change within the house as well as without, and I am as attuned to the rhythm of the year as any farmer or woodsman. Even the kind of dirt I sweep up off the floor differs with the season: grass cuttings in June, for example, sand in midsummer, bits of dead leaf in the fall, and from October through April—mud. This book, then, celebrates the year—the ordinary year in our ordinary house. Our way of life is ordinary, too. We haven't gone to New Guinea nor crossed the Pacific on a raft nor kept a boa constrictor in the bathroom nor raised a chimpanzee in the nursery. The Russians have sent a planet up into space, and as I write this, it is now going seven miles per second and they say it will eventually circle the sun once every fifteen months. We take note of these things and ponder them and are concerned, but I admit that most of the time it is more urgent to decide what to have for dinner, and I think most people's lives are like that.

It is snowing, a peculiar snowfall coming out of a sunny blue sky, sifting down as if manufactured miraculously in mid-air. I've looked out the window, and in the back yard Polly and Jill are dancing about the black cherry that feeds the birds for us each summer. Around and around they go, skipping in a slow, ritual fashion, lifting their arms at regular intervals and then letting them fall. One, two, three, *plop*; one, two, three, *plop*. Around and around, like Black Sambo's tigers, except that their faces are set in fierce, ecstatic, almost druidic contemplation. I have just gone to look again; they're still at it.

I have made my New Year's Resolutions. Any day now I shall start keeping them.

(1) Write this book.
(2) Lose ten pounds . . .

FEBRUARY

FEBRUARY is the shortest month of the year and whoever made it the shortest must have been a man of infinite foresight and mercy because it's not only the shortest month, it's also the worst. Valentine's Day has been put into the middle of February for purposes of relief, but this is more or less like dropping a saccharine tablet into a glass of paraldehyde. February is also crammed with birthdays, so that I suppose it may seem like a good month to some people (like George Washington and my niece Carol, Abraham Lincoln and my aunt Kate), but as far as my personal experience goes February is crammed mostly with other things: mumps, measles, chickenpox, and the common cold.

Malcolm gets at least two cases of acute sinusitis a year and one is always in February. My heart bleeds for him, but Mac is twelve years old and not the most cooperative of patients. My tenderness, solicitude, and sympathy are fine up to a point, but then I have to admit that the Nightingale instinct in me often takes the form of an old crow. "Steam yourself!" I croak, and Mac hangs over the steaming-pan for about 54 seconds, carefully not breathing. "Is that enough?" he asks, just before his lungs collapse. "No, that is *not* enough," I say. Now he has, surreptitiously, drawn a breath, and he uses every cubic centimeter of it. "DO I HAVE TO STAND HERE FOR A THOUSAND MILLION OCTOBILLION YEARS?" he shrieks. "Just ten minutes," I reply with a sweetly murderous smile, "but please *breathe*."

He leans over the pan now and inhales and exhales with magnificent whistling and howling sound effects like an arctic gale: "Shoooeeee-heeeeow! Shoooeeee-heeeeow! SHOOOOEEEE-HEEEOW!"

"The noise," I remark, "is not necessary."

"What do you want me to do, then?" he cries in outrage, and he bends over the pan and pants delicately like a terrified mouse, "Huffa-huffa-huffa-huffa."

"The object," I tell him, straining the words through my incisors, "is simply to breathe the steam in, breathe the steam out. Just breathe."

"I can't!"

"THEN STOP BREATHING, FOR ALL I CARE!"

There is a long, pitiful silence. "You want me to die, or something?" he asks.

This has been going on for nearly a week now, this and similar sessions devoted to baking his sinuses under the infrared lamp, plus trips to the doctor's office for drainage, plus $8 worth of wonder drugs. Finally last night I figured Mac would be more or less fit to go back to school this morning. (I didn't want him to die, I just wanted him to go back to school.) Cameron complained of a slight sore throat yesterday, but that was something I felt I could cope with; so I got up this morning in fairly high spirits, looking forward to a rebirth of freedom, and we all sat down to eat breakfast. "Drink your orange juice," I said, this being part of my brilliant daily breakfast-table repartee ("Drink your orange juice," "Stop fighting!" "Watch that milk bottle!" "One spoonful of sugar is enough," and "MOP IT UP!"), punctuating items of the eight-o'clock news my husband was desperately trying to hear on the radio. (He turns the volume up competitively, decibel by decibel, and when he finally snaps it off in the middle of the fighting or the mopping I never know whether it's because the sports news has begun or because he's decided there's no point trying to maintain contact with the outside world.) At any rate, Cameron, in a rare fit of compliance, lifted up his orange juice, took two swallows, and exploded into tears. I took one look, laid my hand on his forehead, phoned the people across the street to get our thermometer back, unbuttoned his shirt, and confirmed my worst suspicions. He had a temperature of 102° and he was as bright pink as if he'd been sitting in a Japanese bath. Scarlet fever—and nobody could go to school, not any of them. February had struck again.

At this writing the doctor has been here, given Cam a needle in the rear, and prescribed another $8 worth of wonder drugs. Cam is lying in bed upstairs, too sick to be a nuisance, but the other children will have to wait for clearance from the city health inspector before they can go back to school. Wayne has brought home some groceries, ice cream for the patient, and materials for the rest of them to manufacture Valentines out of while they sit around. The gas company man has come to fiddle with the furnace, a little boy has come with a note from Cameron's teacher, the drugstore has delivered the wonder drugs (they ought to call them no-wonder drugs: no wonder our druggist goes to Las Vegas for his vacation), and something seems to be going wrong with the television. I have cleaned up the house with the exception of the Valentine factory in the kitchen, where bits of red paper and lace doily are sifting in an intermittent snowfall to the floor, and now I must lay this aside and type out my notes for tonight's night-school lecture on poetry. I feel as poetic as a discarded tongue depressor or a dirty dustmop, but I must explain the Petrarchan and Shakespearian sonnets, regardless. The Show Must Go On, even in public night school.

I forgot to mention that my northern-exposure clothesline fell down last month and hasn't been put back up yet. I like the climate we have here, but just for once it would have been nice to go out and pick that wet laundry up off some nice clean snow.

One thing cheers me. I think, as I check back and count on my fingers, that we don't have any more of the usual childhood diseases left ahead of us. It was last year (mostly in February, of course) that the younger children had measles, mumps, and chickenpox all in a glorious succession, so now everybody has had everything. Except, I mustn't forget, we still have three sets of tonsils remaining and can always have a good run of tonsillitis.

Actually we're a healthy family, aside from sinuses and a bit of hay fever and a few allergies and a slight tendency toward intestinal flu (better known around here as The Blight). What I mean is, we don't have anybody in an iron lung or a wheelchair, at least not at the moment. We don't even run to broken bones, but only the little girls have escaped stitches so far; the boys, like their shirt elbows and trouser knees, are always in need of mending. Andy is hobbling around right now with about half a dozen stitches in his knee, and Duncan and Malcolm have at one time or another opened up each other's heads. Mac even managed to do a fine solo job once with a claw hammer. I don't know what he was hammering, and he never got it hammered anyway because on the backswing the claw connected with the back of his skull and he came reeling into the house with a shower of blood spattering all over his shoulders. (Malcolm is also the one who tried seesawing with Duncan at a time when Duncan outweighed him by about twenty pounds. He went flying up into the air, dropped head first on the center bar of the seesaw, and had a dandy brain concussion.) Andy walked right into a barbed-wire fence and opened up his forehead a scant half inch above his eye. We were camping on our way to Mexico at the time, and it required a wild 14-mile chase to find a doctor. We finally turned up one who was a full-blooded California Indian—which fact gave the expedition a certain anthropological charm it would otherwise have lacked. At least my anthropologist husband was charmed; *he* actually met the doctor. The rest of us sat in the car in the 93° heat and waited for 1 hour and 45 minutes, wilted and lunchless, while he waved cheerily at us from time to time from the window of the doctor's cool, curtained, air-conditioned office. Cameron once fell on the toy fire engine (the one that is about thirty-five years old and was won by my husband's great-uncle Al on a punchboard) and tore his lip; and Duncan threw Malcolm across the room and tore *his*.

But these are all pleasant memories now; we enjoy them in retrospect and recall them with that certain relish with which everybody seems to recall misfortunes happily survived. Some people, in fact, don't wait for retrospect. We have one friend from whom we hear only in the midst of catastrophe (hers, not ours). Months, even years of silence pass, and then we get a communiqué recounting gleefully how the oil burner exploded, the houseboat cut loose from its moorings, they're out of a job and living on spaghetti, and they owe her mother $85, and how are we? I have been working on a psycho-sociological or maybe socio-psychological analysis of this and think it may have something to do with a firm conviction that one must struggle at all costs to be a permanent underdog. We have tried to imagine what would happen should this friend of ours ever come, oh unfortunately! into a million dollars. We can only conclude that it would ruin her life. It's pretty hard to answer these letters; they always seem to come at a time when we don't have any handy catastrophes of our own. I guess our replies have been, over the years, rather unsatisfactory.

I could have written, had we been corresponding at the time, about Cameron's black eye, which he got at the business end of a baseball bat. Malcolm enters into sports with more enthusiasm than sense; he rarely looks in front of him, and never behind. Behind him, this time, was Cameron, then four years old. Mac swung and Cam went flying across the sidewalk and into the gutter, from which, with a minimum of tears, he arose, dusted himself off, and walked away. He accepted it all so nonchalantly that I barely noticed the event. But by evening his whole head looked bashed out of shape and where he should have had a right eye he had instead a huge, squashed, purplish-red canned plum. Strong men turned pale to see him on the street; even the doctor's nurse cut short an unprofessional moan of horror. When the plum finally began to shrivel, days later, and the actual presence of the eye beneath was confirmed, Cam looked at me candidly, china-blue iris swimming in a lake of perfect crimson, and swore up and down it had never hurt a bit. I don't think, however, that even this could have competed with debt, unemployment, a drifting houseboat, and an exploding oil burner.

A dear little old lady, desiccated and rustly, spoke to me on the bus coming home from night school the other night. Noting my bundle of papers caught up in a manila file-folder, she asked me what I "did." I replied that I taught Creative Writing at night school. "Oh, how lovely!" she cried. "I *do* think it's wonderful that some people are taking an interest in penmanship these days!" I clutched my folder more tightly, trusting that none of the papers protruded far enough for her to see the x'd out, erratic typing on some, the wild (but creative!) scrawls on others, and I smiled nicely through a discourse on the Palmer Method all the way to her stop. The last I saw of her was the farewell flutter of a small, disembodied, fawn-gloved hand in the night.

February is also Virginia's month and not merely because she too, like Lincoln and Washington and the rest, has a birthday in the middle of it. Virginia, who is both the oldest and the newest of our children, arrived one night three years ago in February, with a battered suitcase and a downtrodden look, towed in by a social worker who was careful to tell us (with a weary, wary fatalism) that if things didn't work out we were to let him know. It was only after about a year and a half that he finally stopped asking us, at least once a month, in a gingerly and apprehensive way, whether things were "working out."

I won't pretend that I was filled with boundless optimism when I saw Virginia. In the first place, when I read how hard it was for the Children's Aid Society to find homes for children of mixed racial heritage—particularly Indians—and wrote impulsively to say we would be glad to try being foster parents to such a child, I had in mind a smallish child, perhaps four or five years old. Duncan, our oldest, was then only ten, and little hole-in-the-head Jill was seven months old. I had never been anybody's foster mother but I was least of all prepared to become, overnight, the mother of an adolescent Indian girl half my own age. Nowadays people hardly seem to want their own teen-agers, and to take in somebody else's looked like an act bordering on the unbalanced. A baby or a small child is pliable and can be molded; but what on earth can you do with someone already seventeen years old?

I don't know the answer yet, because as far as I can see we have *done* very little that you can put your finger on. But Virginia has changed so much that it is hard for me to remember what she was like that first night. She struggled through the tenth grade in our high school—and it was really a struggle for a girl from an Indian residential school where the main curricular emphasis seems to have been upon sports, choir singing, and the domestic arts, particularly the art of carefully cutting all the spots out of the potatoes for the staff's supper and carefully leaving them all in for the children's supper. When she finished tenth grade she went to vocational school; and as I write this she has almost completed a year of steady employment in the first shop that hired her, a good record for any young person moving out into the world for the first time, and for Virginia a kind of miracle.

In a few days Virginia will be twenty. Her three years with us have gone quickly, and there were seventeen before them when the twig was bent in other directions. We have kept our hopes moderate and contained. But the downtrodden girl with the battered suitcase is now a young lady with a sparkling eye and a pert manner, a bit of sauciness we privately relish because it means she feels safe here, and sure of herself.

I could use Virginia as the prime support of a wonderful pose, making myself out to be a sort of Great Earth-Mother type, overflowing with warmth and acceptance and superhuman patience, ready to take all the neglected and abandoned children of the world under my wing. But the truth is a far remove. I am *not* a Great Earth-Mother type—I am a harassed, sharp-tongued, absent-minded woman, absorbed in my writing and reading, selfish about my working hours at my desk, an indifferent housekeeper and an erratic cook, and quite capable of shouting at the children, more than once a day, "GET OUT AND LEAVE ME ALONE, WILL YOU?"

I haven't yet decided whether this is a bad thing or possibly a good thing. Perhaps an occasional explosion from a mother who suddenly, inexplicably, doesn't want four neighbor boys joining her own four in a wild scuffle in the living room helps to keep the children in touch with reality. The outside world does not always brim with love and uncritical, undemanding acceptance—why should I? Of course, if home is supposed to be the place where you can get away with murder, and if Mother is supposed to be a soft, cozy Family Rug, then I'm out of step. I've been told by the children that I am harsh, cruel, mean, unfair, and that they never have any fun and aren't allowed to do *anything*. But I notice that when it rains, it seems to be our basement everybody's playing in (and there are so many excellent reasons why they can't play in any other basement); and it's our cedar trees that have the tree-fort, our yard that has swings, rings, and a slide, plus a great patch of dirt where children are allowed to dig to China. (There are all kinds of excellent reasons why no other yard has a place for anybody to dig.) As the meanest parents in the neighborhood, we accumulate the darnedest supply of extra children. There must be a strong streak of masochism in the juvenile personality.

I suspect the main reason we accumulate so many other children is that we have more to start with. Each one of ours attracts his own group of companions, so that on a typical day there may be girls from 3 to 6 feeding dollies on the front porch, boys of 9 and 10 doing things I prefer not to know about (like hanging by their toes from the tree-fort), 12- to 14-year-olds mixing chemical messes in the basement or testing radios up in the radio "shack" in Duncan's closet, and in Virginia's room a giggle of girls trying on dresses, putting hair in pin-curls, and listening to the top twenty tunes on a radio with a constantly up-creeping volume control. Believe me, in the midst of all of this you won't find me beaming fatuously like Cornelia ("*These* are my jewels!"). More likely I'm holding my head while I try to organize the next of my Tuesday-Thursday night-school lectures or try to find a few spare minutes for The Book I Am Supposed to Be Writing.

But perhaps Virginia will feel even better about herself when she reflects in time to come that a woman who was *not* overflowing with the milk of human kindness still found enough love and patience to keep her; for it means, Virginia, that there was something in *you* that made you worth keeping, despite all the deficiencies in *me*.

Cameron is now recuperating from scarlet fever and Malcolm is back in school with the rest of them (except Jill, of course), all bearing written excuses and quarantine release slips. The house is full of red hearts and paper-lace doilies and Cupid stickers. The television set has gone to the repair shop and my vacuum cleaner has finally, unmistakably expired after a protracted illness. Suddenly all the children's clothes are falling apart and I pile up elbowless shirts and kneeless trousers for Virginia's handy, professional touch with the sewing machine. Duncan's shoes are ready to give out, but he refuses to go to the shoe store, having better things to do with his valuable time; he is building himself a telescope. "Oh, they'll last till June," he says, with a scornful look.

Outside, a little bunch of snowdrops blooms by the driveway and green spikes of all kinds are coming up through the ground. Out back, in the adjoining yard, our neighbor Mr. D. comes out with a shovel, and I begin to worry—is there something we ought to be digging, too? A few snowflakes fell yesterday, but they didn't stay; it is perfectly still outside, gray but bright, no snow, no rain, nothing at all. We quiver with expectation—either it will suddenly turn spring or else we will be plunged back into winter. We can only hope; there aren't any groundhogs to let us know. Last year there wasn't any winter at all, but only a long fall and a long spring, without a single flake of snow or any days of icy temperature. We reveled in it (we love to read the weather reports from the East and Midwest, where people are fighting blizzards, hurricanes, floods, tornadoes, droughts, and heat waves 365 days a year), but we paid the price when all the bugs that should have died that winter rose up to confound us. We spent the summer cursing and spraying and trying to get a few vegetables to eat and flowers to look at before They got them. There were 7,865,221 cutworms in the corn patch, and my precious leaf lettuce and chard were reduced to old Belgian lace. I mixed lethal concoctions of various sorts and sprayed furiously and viciously, but nothing stopped them. I lay awake each night, and even in our bedroom I could hear their little jaws munching, munching.

The cutworms filled me with fury, but that is nothing compared to the way I feel about moths. I would rather open a closet and have a full-grown Bengal tiger spring out at me than a half dozen clothes moths. I spend a fortune on anti-moth warfare and I am always positive I have sprayed everything, but there is always a dresser drawer I have forgotten. I'll be glad when they've finished eating everything we own that is made of wool; then I'll starve them to death with all the synthetic inedible unwoolly garments I can buy. Shearman, spare that sheep!

February is half gone now. Our payment booklet has come back from the bank and we owe a mere $7,984 on the house. Out by the back fence the rhubarb is up two and a half inches. It's raining.

Wayne has put my clothesline back up. It is now spliced in two places and the splices won't run through the pulleys, so I have half a clothesline—the shady half. Oh well, nothing will dry out there until July anyway. The children, TV-less, are all in the living room with a book from the library as a guide, practicing Yoga. Jill stands on one foot with her hands above her head, fingertips together, her other foot resting neatly against the top of the opposite thigh; the book says *Vrksasana.* Cameron twists his legs into a pretzel and sits easily with an imperturbable look, but Duncan, having wrestled his size 8 feet into position, immediately loses his balance and rolls over curled up like an armadillo. Nevertheless, it was Duncan who brought the book home, determined to read it all, put it into practice, and live to be 110.

My own desire to practice Yoga is lessened somewhat by the fact that the pilot light in the gas oven went out today. In order to relight it in our gas oven, you must simultaneously hold the lighted match to the pilot (this calls for lying on the floor with your arm in the broiler) and depress something called the Oventrol which some male gorilla masquerading as an industrial designer put up on top with the other controls so that you need arms twice as long as normal to reach it and the pilot at the same time (I am 5 ft. 3½ in. tall and not built so that I can shamble along with my knuckles scraping the ground), and you must press it in hard for a full minute, all the while keeping your eye on the gas and your ear, consequently, against the linoleum. I kept weakening, the pilot kept blinking out, and I was lying there surrounded by about half a cord of burnt matches before success (and a sprained shoulder) were mine. Who needs Yoga exercises from a book?

I'd like to put that stove designer in the same place I'd like to put the man who designed the refrigerator we have with a lovely egg rack on the door. It has holes for *nine* eggs.

It is still raining.

Duncan has performed an autopsy on the vacuum cleaner. The cause of death remains unknown but the possibility of revival has been eliminated; its liver and lights lie strewn from one end of the basement workbench to the other. This may not seem like progress to you, but in my heart of hearts I'm grateful. I've never liked vacuum cleaners anyway, even at peak performance. In fact, I don't like any household equipment that makes a noise; I'd rather get a sore arm making an angel-food cake than listen to the snarling whir of the electric beater. And when, on a Sunday afternoon, the neighborhood vibrates with the whine and roar of power mowers, I grow nostalgic for summer evenings long ago and the faraway sound of a lawn being cut the old-fashioned way. It was a lovely sound that mingled with the summer air as if it belonged.

It is raining even harder.

A question keeps coming into my mind and I might as well own up to it, even if I intend (in the long run) to go blithely on and ignore it. The question is, why am I writing this book?

I haven't any idea and I don't suppose I'll know even when I've finished. It does occur to me that when my children grow up they might want to know what they were like. It also occurs to me that they might find out what their Mother was like, but that's a risk I've got to take.

Of course, they may remember perfectly, anyway. Some people remember everything. People who write their memoirs are blessed with prodigious memories for rooms in houses they have not seen since they were two years old; they recall all the details of a cousin's birthday party in 1925; and they remember not only events and objects but also, with stunning precision, emotions and states of mind both habitual and occasional. "I was a cheerful, happy child, fond of fun and games," they say, or, "I was a morose, moody creature, given to tantrums . . ." Of course, some of this may be secondhand, repetitions of what other people have told them about themselves. Still, by the time a man sits down to write his memoirs, people who were adults when he was a child are not usually available for conference.

(Or if they are, I can imagine the scene: "What kind of child was I?" the would-be author asks his aged auntie. "Eh?" she says. "WHAT KIND OF CHILD WAS I?" he asks again, loudly and carefully. "Oh," she answers, "you were a happy, cheerful child . . . or was that your brother George? Come to think of it, you were a morose, moody creature, given to tantrums . . .")

I hardly remember a thing. I do remember eating a handful of salty ice by mistake from the back of a delivery truck, and I remember getting into the big jar of fig-and-senna balls my mother kept for what ailed us. I also remember the night the roof leaked and the plaster fell all over the living room. I remember a boat trip when I was eight; no, I don't exactly remember the trip but I do remember stepping off the boat, missing the dock and opening my eyes underwater to see the still-turning propeller blades inches from my nose. But my fond recollections, aside from being rather alarmingly fixed upon catastrophe, don't have any real teeth in them until my junior high school days and even then it's astonishing how much of my life has vanished without a trace.

However, I do have (or did have, until recently) a kind of general impression of myself as a child, an impression which filled in the unknown, eventless days with something, at least. What kind of child was I? Well, I thought, I was a morose, moody creature; not given to tantrums, but at least given to sulking and skulking in corners. Given to hiding my head in a book from morn to night. Friendless. Not the outgoing type. Not adjusted, you might say. I was terrible at games, and rather despised them anyway.

That, in brief, was my mental image of myself as a young child—a rather unpleasant image, but it does explain later intellectual pretensions, social disabilities, and my stubborn refusal at parties to go down to the basement and play ping-pong. In a way, I cherished it.

But when we moved into the house where we live now, a lot of things I hadn't looked at in years came to light, and among them was an old diary of mine, written in the year I was ten. Where were the peevish private remarks of a misunderstood and maladjusted child? "It snowed today," I had written on a Thursday in January. And on Friday, "Gee, I wish it was Saturday because there is a good snow and the hill will be keen!" And on Saturday, gleefully, "Almost killed myself sliding!" On Sunday? "Gee, I'm mad! The rain came and spoiled all the sliding!"

But it snowed again. In fact, for this mild corner of the world it was a pretty snowy winter, and oh boy did I have fun sliding—pages and pages of sliding. Where was the morose, moody creature, the unhappy girl with her nose in a book, who had to be cajoled and threatened to get her out of the house and into the fresh air?

Well, I sat there with my diary for a long time, reading about the snow and the sliding and the daily condition of the hill, and at last I had to see myself, mittened and mufflered, cherry-nosed and apple-cheeked, shouting and puffing great frosty January breaths, having a wonderful time.

I was a cheerful, happy child . . .

So, dear children of mine, if any of you are afflicted with memories like sieves, this book will be a kind of refresher; you will know what kind of children you were. I also recommend it to future daughters-in-law: dear girls, never let them tell you what a perfect housekeeper Mother was, nor what a superb cook. Read and you will know better. I give you my love and best wishes.

It is never going to stop raining.

Duncan's shoes have fallen apart and he had to wear sneakers (or running shoes, *runners* for short, as they call them here) to school yesterday; he was quite astonished, naturally. But it doesn't matter anyway because he's up in bed running a temperature of 102°. Malcolm, who went as usual to have his sinuses drained yesterday and stopped by Dr. King's to have his hemoglobin tallied up, has turned out to be anemic. He started a course of iron tablets last night and wound up with an upset stomach, so he's up there in bed too. This leaves me at my usual February occupation, hauling trays, thermometer, pills, glasses of juice, newspapers, etc., etc., etc., up and down the stairs. The Book I Am Supposed to Be Writing is lying on my desk, gathering dust, along with a half-dozen manuscripts from the aspiring students of my Tuesday-Thursday creative writing class, a thick sheaf of junk clipped together and labeled INCOME TAX, and a little letter from four schoolchildren in Great Neck, Long Island, asking me (among other things), "Are there any bad things about being a writer?" Should I tell them?

Duncan just called me upstairs; he didn't want anything except to know why we don't move to New York City. He was mooning over the Sunday *Times*, which we get a week late out here, and showed me the notice of a series of lectures called "Great Heretics," sponsored by some foundation whose honorary president is Bertrand Russell. Heresy appeals to Duncan; he has been, in a general way, heretical since the age of six.

The sun is struggling to come out but I don't care. It's

still February for a few days yet and I'm sure nothing really good can happen until it's over.

Jill has just come to the door to ask if she can have her swim suit on. It seems the Hugheses' driveway is flooded and she thinks it would make a dandy swimming pool. She's crying because I said no, beast that I am.

Things are bound to get better as soon as March is here. I think the smart thing for me to do is just to go away and wait for March 1.

February 28: I can't help it, I have to tell you. I just broke my glasses.

MARCH

I AM ALWAYS a year older in March, but this depresses me less than it probably should. I ought to be wild with despair, for each March comes more quickly on the heels of the previous one (a sort of quick March?) until I am about to be thirty-seven without ever becoming used to being thirty-six. In fact, I can never remember how old I am without remembering first what year it is and then subtracting 1922 from it.

I've never lied about my age, but I give the undoubted appearance of lying about it. At least three times I have, in the course of radio talks for the Canadian Broadcasting Corporation, referred gaily or wistfully or defensively to my age—my age at the time, that is. Unfortunately, these talks are generally recorded on tape and reach the air months and months later, and then sometimes they appear in print, even later than that. It was just the other day I was in the Nelson *Daily News* (British Columbia's Most Interesting Newspaper) referring to myself as having reached the ripe old age of thirty-three, when in fact I am about to reach the ripe old age of thirty-seven.

Actually I don't mind the inexorable progression of the years, even though it is obvious that time is passing a lot faster than it used to. It was only ten years ago that a month seemed quite long, perhaps because halfway through each one we always ran out of money and the second half thereupon became twice as long as the first. Now I just barely get the bank statements balanced and the first-of-the-month bills paid and suddenly it's the end of the month and time to start all over again. Months are bad enough, but days have become negligible units of time, barely worth considering; specific days melt away like snowflakes brought into the kitchen for inspection. As for the week, it's not much better. When I'm teaching Tuesday and Thursday at night school, all my weeks have no middles at all; there's Monday one day, then Friday, and then the weekend. It's no wonder I'm getting to be thirty-seven so fast.

Despite my advanced years I still wear shorts or pedal pushers most of the time and probably will go on wearing them until I am sitting in a wheelchair with a lavender shawl thrown about my shoulders. (Will a lavender shawl look well with plaid calf-length trousers and a cardigan sweater, when I'm ninety-seven?) However, I have capitulated in one respect, and appear in public (at least on Tuesday and Thursday nights) in decorous heels, nylons, a neat Empire sheath or a straight skirt and sweater. This hasn't been easy, mind you; sometimes as I walk along the street I catch a sudden glimpse of a reflection in a store window, and who is that dressed like a tidy middle-class matron with P.T.A. and SUPERMARKET branded on her forehead? Lord, it's *me!*

Whoever me may be, that is.

I've always wanted to be the kind of mother whose kids come in at 3:30 from school, cold and wet and hungry, and find cups of hot chocolate waiting, and freshly baked cookies, and the house smelling of cinnamon and love. The trouble is I also want to be a writer, so they're just as likely to come home and find nothing at all but the sound of the typewriter and my snarling voice, "Fix yourself a peanut-butter sandwich and WASH THE KNIFE AFTERWARDS!"

And that's not all, either. I have several images of myself and I can't choose among them. I lay claim, in fact, to being the most remarkable, hitherto-undiscovered, long-standing, and untreated case of split personality on record. Come to think of it, since up to this moment my case has not been on record, I hereby put it on record. Medical journals please copy.

Mine is no ordinary case; each day it strikes me afresh. It begins with the first drowsy moments of awakening, as I knock the howling alarm clock under the bed and grab it just as it begins to crawl away from me into the dust. At last, with its dying gasps still rattling my tympanic membranes like hail on a corrugated tin roof, I lie back on the pillow, stabbing myself critically at the base of the skull with the one bobby pin I didn't find last night, and a cold thought clutches me around the heart. *Who am I?*

Sickly, knowing I must face it, I haul myself to my feet and stare into the full-length mirror; but there is no answer there, only a strange almost-thirty-seven-year-old woman in yellow baby-dolls. Shuddering, I wrench open the closet door and feel myself shattering not into two parts but into a kind of psychological chowchow.

Which am I? The matron in the tweed skirt, nylons, and medium-heel pumps? Or a slightly overmature teen-ager in the plaid pedal pushers and the Peter Pan blouse? A *femme fatale* in black matador pants, a gold shirt, and glass beads? or a comfy Mom in a drip-dry gingham house dress and flatties?

It's pretty silly when a woman of thirty-seven (almost) hasn't made up her mind what she is or what she wants to be. It might be easier if I could organize a sort of day-by-day rotation; but that won't work—there are too many of me and sometimes they all want in at once. Talk about Eve White, Eve Black, and Miss Sensible Compromise whatever-her-name-was; why, the three of them don't have a patch on me. I shift from one character to another so fast and so often that I've got the only case of split personality with stripped gears.

Maybe on Tuesday at 3:30 I'm amiable, placid, and agreeable, the kind of plump, smiling, aproned Mom for whom those hideous satin pillows that say MOTHER on them must be intended. But if I am amiable, placid, and agreeable on Tuesday, then on Wednesday the house is a mess and amiable, placid, agreeable Mom vanishes in a puff of smoke, leaving a raging fiend who races through the house with broom and dustpan, groveling under the beds for wadded-up socks, trying to find all thirty-one chessmen (I've given up on that sixteenth pawn; we use anything that's handy) and sliding about on marbles, dinky toys, and bits of construction sets.

Meanwhile another me is pleading for emergence—an elegant me, with her hair done every week and polish on her nails. She wants to sit by the record player, drinking liqueur and listening to chamber music, and laughing low in her throat like an amused jaguar while the dust piles up behind the davenport. (*Her* children spend their afternoons at the neighbors', making cinnamon toast and covering somebody else's kitchen linoleum with granulated sugar. *She* doesn't have to flog some reluctant scholar through a page of long division, nor help construct a flour-salt clay relief map of Palestine, nor read aloud *The Sing-Song of Old Man Kangaroo* when she has a sore throat.)

Still another me keeps a house with invisible windowpanes, where the copper gleams softly and the leaves of the potted plants are all hand-polished every one. When she bakes a cake she must bolt it to the table lest it float away and mash its frosting roses on the ceiling. People ask her for her recipes and she laughs, lightly, saying it's merely a dab of this and a dab of that. But when one of her beautifully behaved, civilized children slams the kitchen door so emphatically that a guest finds a splinter of glass in his *Boeuf à la Flamande,* she becomes unreasonable and may go away to sulk for as much as three weeks at a time, which is long enough to live on macaroni and cheese, hot dogs, and canned baked beans.

These are only a few of me; there are others. (For example, the romantically lovely me in a peignoir like the ones in the ads—you know the ones I mean, where the lady stands there swathed in three or four acres of chiffon and she's holding something up and looking at it as if it were a bouquet of orchids or an autographed photograph of Rossano Brazzi only when you look closely you discover it's a roll of toilet paper?) But these are enough to make me spend my days in bewilderment, confusion, and frustration. The trouble with my split personality is that there isn't a single one of the fragments big enough to take over for a reasonable length of time. Even if I think I've started out properly in the morning, I'm all mixed up by noon. For example, there I go again down the street, looking like a suburban housewife on her way to the supermarket, while wild lines of poetry surge through my head and a candle gutters on the lonely checkered tablecloth of my heart. Under these circumstances who can choose between seven brands of detergent? Who can decide which cereal box contains the novelty least likely to cause civil war at the breakfast table? Who can think of something to have for dinner on Wednesday?

This can't go on. Why can't I be Miss Sensible Compromise? Somewhere, buried deep, there must be a Real Me, somewhere an identity inhabitable for twenty-four hours a day, seven days a week.

I saw Salvador Dali once on television and I have never forgotten something he said. "Every day," said he, "I try to be a little more Dali." There, I thought, *he* knows who he is; lucky Salvador! I could never hope to grow such an elegantly preposterous mustache, but if only I could, every day, be a little more me. . . .

But me *who?*

Duncan is still home in bed, coughing over a mountain of homework. But the flowering plum up the street is ready to burst every purplish bud with the first full sunny day and it isn't February any longer. I wonder how much new glasses will cost?

Are there any bad things about being a writer? Oh, brother. First of all, there are those nine unfinished book-length manuscripts. I always get up to page 47 or page 85 and then something goes wrong. If I could just put all those beginnings together I'd come out with at least two complete books, but unfortunately none of them matches up very well with any of the others. There are two about

Indians, but one's a children's book and the other isn't; there are two about anthropologists, but one's a sorrowful little comedy and the other isn't; there's one about . . . Oh, this is too terrible; I can't go on with this catalogue. The worst is The Book I Am Supposed to Be Writing, which has a dandy opening chapter—and then no more.

Aside from all this, I have a pile of half-written short stories, outlines for short stories, three-sentence résumés of proposed short stories, and disjointed notes for short stories. I work at these sporadically, but I am constantly torn between the kind of stories that make money and the kind of stories I enjoy writing. Editors do not want to pay for stories about aged Indians (no "reader identification"), nor about old maids ("unattractive"), nor about people who have trouble scraping up the down payment on a house ("too depressing"), nor about people who think (too "interior"). On the other hand, I have written for the magazines so many stories about pregnant women that when I feed a piece of paper into the typewriter I get an attack of morning sickness. I've written stories about women wanting babies and not having them, having them and not wanting them, wanting them, having them, and then losing them. Pregnant women are obviously big in the fiction field.

I want to break out of this, get into something new. That's why right now I'm working on a science-fiction story called *Yonder Star*, with rocket ships and distant planets and all that sort of thing. Funny thing, though—woman in it has a baby.

Pass the Gravol, please.

Virginia has just come to me with a long list of words: would I please tell her what they mean? I took the list cheerfully and then cried, "My God, *what* are you reading?"

"The Kinsey Report," she said.

I gave her the definitions.

Do you know that the quickest way to get rid of a hungry child is to tell him that dinner will be ready in ten minutes and he ought to wash his hands? The child will then disappear for 45 minutes to 1½ hours.

There's a lot that's not getting into this book. Malcolm joined the Junior Forest Wardens, for example, and Andy wants to go to San Juan Island when Easter comes so he can hunt rabbits with his bow and arrow; Malcolm has been going down to the Indian reserve Saturdays to dig with the university archaeology club, and Jill has been singing "Red red red is the color of my true love's hair" with undentable egocentricity. But I don't want to make this book too long; I've never liked great big books anyway. *Gone With the Wind* and *Anthony Adverse* just aren't my favorites; I prefer things the size of *The Bridge of San Luis Rey* or *Ethan Frome*. Besides, the essence of art is selectivity. Take this new family I've been hearing about for the past few weeks. The older boys have been in the throes of an infatuation with this particular family and we've heard all about the boat they own, the things they do, how they just love children and never tell them to go away, and what fascinating lives they lead. They even have a stuffed black bear cub in the living room. All these facts came out easily, but it took adroit prying to dislodge this additional fact: they may have a stuffed black bear cub in the living room, but they *don't have television.*

Children are true and natural artists.

If I can find that little blue Vest Pocket Calorie Counter book I know is somewhere around the house, I will start dieting. I don't have much time to look for it, though.

My children are beginning to look like charity cases. Polly still has two dresses that fit, but the buttons on the suspenders of her two pleated skirts have been lowered until they hang by a thread from the very ends—and the skirts still look short. Wayne's one good suit isn't going to be able to bear up under the light of a sunny spring day. I don't know why, but clothing is something I've never been able to work neatly into our budget. I can dress the eight of us (Virginia buys her own clothes) on about $500 a year, a sum that allows me two pairs of shoes and has kept me in the same bathing suit since 1954. Sometimes I read about women who spend more than our entire family income on clothing for themselves alone. It fascinates me, because when I go shopping I can't even find something I like among the clothes I *can't* afford. Gradual affluence, assisted by inflation, has brought me from $5.98 through $10.98 up to $19.98 as a more or less usual price to pay for a dress (I don't get a dress every year, though). But I don't find any more dresses I like at $19.98 than I used to find at $5.98, and I suspect I wouldn't do much better at $199.98. I just don't see eye to eye with dress designers any more than I do with gorilla-armed stove designers and refrigerator designers who think nine eggs make a dozen.

Anyway, that $500 for clothes is never really *in* the budget, and everybody needs something right now. Moreover, if I wash those bedroom curtains with the kitten eyes on them, they will fall into shreds in the machine—if the machine doesn't fall into shreds first. I spent hours this morning darning great holey socks; I suspect some of the boys have mice living in their shoes.

Personally I loathe the eat-it-up, wear-it-out, make-it-do, do-without philosophy. I make a lot of things do, of course, like my handleless saucepan, but that's as much out of stubbornness as it is out of economy. But you can't always choose your philosophy of life; sometimes it's just there. It comes with the circumstances, and you either accept it or spend your days banging your fool head against the wall. And eat-it-up, wear-it-out, make-it-do, do-without just naturally comes along with six children. I fight back a little by making some money on my own initiative and by spending part of it irrationally. I think everybody should spend a little money irrationally, even people who have hardly any money at all. Man cannot live by bread alone, nor by saucepans, socks, and indoor plumbing. Consider the choice between a grand piano and a matched set of bathroom fixtures in pale pink: after all, a person can sit at a grand piano for hours on end, and that's *music.*

The best appointment I can get with the oculist is for March 24. I've tried to hang the things together (they broke over the nose) with adhesive tape braced with a section of matchstick, but the two lenses keep getting out of line and I end up with a headache. There's no point just getting new frames; the lenses look as if I've been playing tick tack toe on them with a diamond ring (I don't have a diamond ring), and besides I'm pretty sure I need a new prescription. Either that or they're growing trees without separate leaves these days and all the shingles on the roofs in this neighborhood have melted and run together.

The morning concert is on and music fills the house. "Whose music is that?" asks Jill. "Darius Milhaud," I tell her. "Oh," says Jill, "it sounds like that other guy—you know—Beethoven."

It doesn't, but after all what can you expect from a 3½-year-old?

Mac is the real family music lover. Believe me, it is

soul-satisfying to have a boy you can give Haydn quartets to for his twelfth birthday, and Bruckner's Ninth for Christmas. The strange thing about it is that you'd never suspect, for he is the dirtiest, grubbiest, least aesthetic-looking, redheaded, freckle-faced boy ever to be approximated on a *Saturday Evening Post* cover. I may be, for all I know, the only woman in North America who (under pressure) baked a large cake last December 16, wrote "188" on it in confectioner's icing, and carried it to the table singing "Happy Birthday to you, Happy Birthday to you, Happy Birthday dear Ludwig, Happy Birthday to you!" We also read *Peanuts*, so you can divide the honors between Beethoven and Schulz.

I like: Bach, Beethoven, Brahms, Bruckner, Boccherini, Monteverdi and Moussorgsky and Mozart, Prokofiev and Palestrina, Sibelius and Strauss (mostly Richard), Verdi, Wagner, and Vivaldi. At least those come alliteratively to mind, but as a matter of fact the composer of my favorite symphony didn't get on that quick list because I can't think of any other N's besides him, so he will have to stand by himself: Carl Nielsen of Denmark, whose First Symphony gives me gooseflesh of delight.

I don't like: Chopin. I'm sorry. I've tried, but I just can't.

I also don't like: all French art songs.

But I do like: nearly all folk songs, mouth-music from the Hebrides, bagpipes, Gregorian chants, and *anything* played on a drum.

March has come in not like a lion but like a low-down, sneaky, double-crossing snake. Duncan was sitting here looking as if he might be able to go back to school in a day or two when suddenly he began to shake like a nervous fox terrier and I sent him tottering back upstairs to bed again. I followed with the trusty thermometer (we've hung on to it) and plunked it into his mouth after I'd shaken it down properly. Over the years I've developed a pretty handy touch with a thermometer, and I must say I was disgusted with myself when I took it out to read it and kept rotating and peering, rotating and peering, trying to see the mercury column. Then I realized the mercury was filling the whole darned thermometer, right up past 105°. I thundered down the stairs again, crying havoc, and phoned for the doctor, but the doctor had gone curling, so I phoned the curling rink and the doctor hadn't got there yet. I gave them our number and ran back upstairs with two aspirin tablets and a glass of water. Then the doctor phoned from the curling rink and said he would get hold of somebody who could get out here faster than he could. I sent Malcolm whooping across the street for rubbing alcohol from our on-borrowing-terms neighbors (we have a brisk and more or less reciprocal trade in such items as rubbing alcohol, children's aspirin, cough syrup, Kaopectate, and antiphlogistine poultice or "Denver mud") and sat sponging poor shuddering blurry Duncan for an eternity of approximately twelve minutes until a young doctor arrived with penicillin and reassurance. It was *not* pneumonia, only the flu and our old friends the sinuses (those are a few holes in the head I could do without). Anyway, Duncan is bedded down now and his temperature is slowly dropping. The doctor left three days' dosage of oral penicillin he found in his bag—God bless Manufacturer's Samples.

If any more children get sick I am going to turn in my Motherhood badge.

After all, it *is* March, the flowers are blooming, and

Cameron came rushing in yesterday to say, "We ought to be proud! We've got the first dandelion in the whole block!" People have no business being sick.

I see on my memo pad that I must find ten buttons for Polly to take to school; send the draperies to the cleaner; use up the rest of the stuff in the freezer; make sure Mac gets his booklet on igneous rock done for science by March 16; type some papers for Wayne; wash my long and loathsome hair; go to open house at the elementary school tomorrow.

The big problems of life are never as irritating as these floods of trivia. Sometimes I'd trade a list like that for a broken leg.

Must remember to take that rubbing alcohol back, too.

It was, of course, pouring on the school's open-house day. I expected somebody in a turban to come pounding at the door to tell me that the dam had burst, but nobody came except Polly, home for lunch and a complete change of clothing down to the skin. My neighbor and I wound up taking a taxi four blocks to the school, 65 cents and well worth it, as I can't swim and don't even own an umbrella. (I guess I *am* eccentric after all; nearly thirty-seven years old, born, bred and resident in the Pacific Northwest and never owned an umbrella. I hate the things.) Anyway, once we were there I watched Miss B. snappily and enthusiastically putting the sixth-graders of Andy's class through a parsing exercise. It was just like a bunch of lions leaping through flaming hoops; I was astonished that they did it at all, and to see them doing it cheerfully was dazzling. Mrs. D., in Polly's Grade One, exhibited a remarkable ability to make Dick and Jane and Sally and Tim and Spot and Puff quite interesting, and by the time I left her classroom I had begun to think more highly of our creaky educational system.

Then I went to Miss K.'s fourth-grade class, where Cameron and his classmates were reading *Wind in the Willows*. (I don't know *Wind in the Willows;* all I know is that Disneyland has a Mr. Toad's Ride that is, according to the boys, "real neat." When other children were reading *Wind in the Willows* I was reading Eugène Sue's *The Mysteries of the People, or, History of a Proletarian Family Across the Ages*, or maybe Marcy's *Stories of the Cave People,* a handsome blue volume with a good solid socialist moral to every chapter.) Little Sandra got up to read Mr. Toad's speech to his friends Badger, Mole, and Rat. Miss K. made a face. "Really, Sandra," she scoffed lightly, "is *that* how a drunk talks?" (How was Sandra supposed to know? I wondered. Observing at home?) Sandra read it over again with hopeful dramatics. In the back of the room there were smothered sounds from a row of parents. "Mr. Toad is the victim of a disease, class," said Miss K., "a disease that comes out of a bottle. What is it, class?" "Poison?" said somebody. "Oh, dear me," said Miss K., her mouth pulled down. Somebody else whispered timidly. "Well, speak up," said Miss K. forcefully. "What are we afraid of? That's right, he drinks. Mr. Toad is a *drunk!*"

I liked Miss K.

We have decided we *will* go to San Juan Island for the Easter Weekend, to see Nana and Dada and to let Andy try his hand at hunting rabbits with his bow and arrow. Clever children, to have grandparents who live on an island where there are rabbits! There are so many rabbits on San Juan Island, in fact, that I'm sure nobody cares what you hunt them with, short of hand grenades and flame throwers. I don't think Andy will hit one, anyway. I hope I have my glasses before we go. It's a five-hour trip, half by car and half by ferry, and when we leave Anacortes to thread through the most beautiful islands in North America, I want to see something more than blurry, featureless humps floating in the salt water of Georgia Strait.

It's noon. Jill is sitting in the kitchen working on her lunch after spending the morning out playing in mud puddles. I've cleaned up the weekend wreckage, washed my hair, and struggled through the typing of one of those manuscripts for Wayne, translations of Japanese anthropology papers that he has been slowly and painfully editing. This one was physical anthropology and full of fascinating sentences like "The Ainu face has a large bizygomatic maximum diameter (♂ 137.8 ± 0.84 mm), and is mesoprosopic with a rather small total facial index (♂ 87.8 ± 0.51). The naso-frontal suture shows a sharp depression . . ." at which point I find myself showing signs of a rather sharp depression too, especially at the prospect of typing five more manuscripts.

On top of that, I spent hours in the kitchen with all six kids, each one furiously busy on some project. I supervised a book report on *Gulliver's Travels*, Mac's booklet on igneous rocks, Polly's writing of a memorized poem on crocuses, and so on, until I began to fear that the children would become as hopelessly confused as I was. I visualized Duncan turning in a poem on crocuses while Mac wrote about Gulliver and Polly laboriously spelled out i-g-n-e-o-u-s.

Over the weekend I also discovered my little calorie book nestling in a rear corner of my desk drawer. I wasn't looking for it, I was looking for gummed reinforcements, but I found it anyway. Just my luck.

It took me 45 minutes this morning to figure out how to make a presentable meal of what was in the house, in order to avoid going shopping. So I've made a Jello salad with apples and carrots in it, and spiced some canned pears and put them to chill. I guess the main dish will be a kind of shepherd's pie—which Malcolm will doubtless refuse to eat.

An infallible sign of approaching middle age: you get a lump in your throat when they sing one of those medleys, even if there's not a song in it you ever cared a fig for, back when they (and you) were new. You never know, either, what's going to do it to you. I can sit stonily dry-eyed through "Stardust" and "Deep Purple" and then disintegrate at the first few notes of something like "Tip-toe Through the Tulips."

The children have come back from the public library with a feast of books—Cameron with books on stamp collecting and geography, Mac with the life story of a raccoon and a book on seashells, Duncan with *The Age of Ideology,* Freud's *The Meaning and Interpretation of Dreams,* a general psychology text, and something else overwhelming on philosophy. (Well, I remember the boy I idolized when I was in high school. Like many another boy during the reading period he used to prop open his American history text with another book hidden inside it. But his secret treasure was Spinoza.) Duncan won't read every word of all of these, but he does read *at* them. The children once overheard one librarian say to another, "I don't *like* the books that boy takes out," but nobody has crossed him up yet. Things were different when I was young. It took me three tries and three different librarians to get *Ethan Frome* out of our public library. What if those first two librarians had known that I'd already read *The Well of Loneliness* and Havelock Ellis, right on our own library shelves at home?

We did take Andy's collection of comic books away from him in the middle of last year, when it became apparent that he was too lazy to read anything with *words* in it. (He had even goofed a couple of times while making airplane models because he tried to do it all from the pictures, instead of reading the instructions.) So I stored all his comics in the back of my wardrobe and told him he could have them back after he'd done some real reading. Grudgingly he began getting science fiction and juvenile mysteries from the library. In a few weeks I found I had to go upstairs at night and tell him to turn off his light and go to sleep; and one day Cameron came in to tell me that Andy had walked all the way home from school with a book open in front of him, reading as he went. He had read twenty-nine books before he asked for his comics back—and when he got them he discovered they weren't very interesting anyway.

I wasn't the least concerned that his reading was all, exclusively, science fiction and mysteries. Duncan began that way, soon ran out of juvenile science fiction, started on the adult shelf and polished *it* off (including H. G. Wells and others), and promptly turned to psychology, philosophy, and physics. Besides, I like science fiction myself. I wish I could believe that the flying saucers really *have* landed. Somewhere out there, I think they have.

Malcolm indeed loathed the shepherd's pie but everybody else raved about it. Recipe: look in cupboard and moan with despair (there is nothing there but a can of green lima beans, a can of cream of chicken soup, a can of whole kernel corn). Make a biscuit crust, precook three old diced carrots, dump in the beans, corn, soup, put on a top crust, and bake. Pretend you intended it to be that way. Serve with a flourish.

"I like you better with a dress on," Jill says. "Why?" I ask. "Because when you put your pants on," Jill says, "you move too fast."

I must have that washing machine fixed. I am beginning to think of that oil on the floor as a puddle of its lifeblood.

I mentioned curling a few pages back, and if you are at all like me (ignorant) you may have had the same reaction I had the first time anyone said curling to me: "*What*ling?" I exclude people living in Minnesota, New Hampshire, and Vermont, as I am given to understand that they curl, too. Curling, I have discovered from reading the sports page, is an improbable game played on ice by teams of four players, using brooms and big flat stones. The stones go slithering across the ice and the players skate ahead of the stones, sweeping like mad housewives. Curling is an amateur sport and it isn't hard to imagine why. There's just something about those brooms . . .

March 25: Happy Birthday to Me! I am now thirty-seven years old, but I will feel seventy-three until I pick up my new glasses, which the optometrist has promised for tomorrow afternoon. I wish eyes were something you could take out and put in a glass of water, like false teeth. But the children gave me a new lipstick and a new eyebrow pencil, a roll of scotch tape (don't laugh!), pencils, and an eraser. Wayne gave me a sweater, and Virginia must have spent Tuesday and Thursday nights for the past several weeks working on her gift—a new dress that fits perfectly and suits me to a T. I never suspected a thing!

Easter Weekend is upon us. The Japanese manuscripts are all edited, typed, and mailed. My night-school lectures are over for the season. Nobody is sick. I love my new glasses; I can even tell whether it's the right bus in time to get on it! We leave for San Juan Island tomorrow.

And the weekend was a howling success, with weather good enough for clam digging, mountain climbing, and an outdoor Easter Egg Hunt. As for the rabbit hunting. . . well, they decided to go rabbit hunting on Easter morning. It was bright and windy, and the four boys went together, Andy armed with bow and arrows and instructions to shoot only when all three of the boys were well behind him. In an hour they were back. Malcolm came in first, and said to Jill, "Here comes Peter Cottontail, Jilly!" I froze with horror, wondering if Andy had indeed shot a rabbit and would confront Jill with it. In they came, and they *did* have a rabbit. He was sitting in one of their Easter baskets with just his ears sticking out, a little grayish bunny with big dark eyes. They had come across the mother rabbit; some hunter had wounded her and then hadn't found her, and she had run back to her burrow and died near it. There, hopping in circles around her body, was the baby rabbit. He couldn't have been more than four weeks old, perhaps less. Most of the rabbits hadn't even had their litters yet, not until April.

Andy—the Big Rabbit Hunter—tenderly brought the lively bunny all the way home in the Easter basket. How would he have felt if he *had* shot a rabbit?

Everything was in order when we got home. Our neighbor's boy, armed with our house key, had fed Pepper and Muff (our dog and cat), watered the house plants, and brought in the newspapers and the mail. Right on top of the mail was the following, printed on embossed stationery:

> The Social Register of Canada is pleased to announce that your name has been placed before its Committee of Arbiters and accepted for inclusion in its forthcoming edition. The selection of your name and those of the members of your immediate family has been initiated by arbiters who are considered eminently qualified to evaluate the social precedence of the citizens of your community.
>
> The Social Register of Canada is dedicated to honouring those of Canada's citizens whose social prestige is an irrefutable warrant that they or their forebears have contributed significantly to her development.
>
> The Social Register of Canada has been distributed, not only in Canada, but abroad. This and future editions will perpetuate the social prestige of those whose names shall presently be inscribed by continuing to list their names and those of their children generation after generation wherever they may reside.
>
> To ensure accuracy of your listing in the forthcoming edition, you are requested to amplify the biographical data currently available to us by filling in the enclosed biographical form. This we urge you to do at your earliest convenience as, for purposes of editorial clarity, only those entries submitted with complete biographical information will be contained in the forthcoming edition.

We find ourselves dreadfully torn; the impulse to fill in the biographical form (Clubs? I am not much of a joiner, but I never turned in the magic decoding ring that I used to decipher secret messages in those Ovaltine commercials, so I guess I still belong to the Little Orphan Annie Club) vies with the impulse to point out, more soberly, that their eminently qualified arbiters should at least weed us Yankees out of their list, regardless of our social precedence.

I've just looked up "precedence" in the dictionary. "*Pre-ced' ence:* A preceding; priority in time, importance, or esp. rank; specif., ceremonial priority or order; the order observed by persons of different rank on ceremonial occasions." That sounds a little like seating chiefs at a potlatch, and I don't know where *we* come in. I prefer avoiding ceremonial occasions at all costs, so our social precedence has probably never really been put to the test. No, I take that back. Last time we were at an Indian winter spirit dance we were invited to eat in the first shift (boiled elk, vegetables, potatoes, two kinds of pie, and chocolate cake). Do you suppose the Committee of Arbiters was watching?

But even there, I think we may have been below the salt.

APRIL

WHEN THAT *Aprille with his shoures sote* . . .

April always reminds me of Chaucer, and Chaucer reminds me of my lopsided, incomplete, shaky education. What I know about Chaucer you could put into a gnat's ear and he'd never notice it. The same is true of what I know about Plato, Homer, Vergil, and even *Lorna Doone.* I read Adam Smith's *The Wealth of Nations* and Henry George's *Progress and Poverty* when I was in the tenth grade, but I never read *Kidnapped* or *Silas Marner.* I read Edward Bellamy's *Looking Backward* and Jack London's *Martin Eden,* but I never got around to *Vanity Fair,* and though I've tried countless times I've never been able to get past Chapter 2 of A *Tale of Two Cities.* I haven't read

Ben Hur or *Beowulf* or Boccaccio. Fourteen years ago a friend gave me a beautifully boxed volume of Dante and I haven't read that either.

Once in a while in a fit of self-improvement I get out a handy little pocket book I have, called *Good Reading*, and start checking through for all the things I should have read in the thirty-one years I've been literate. I start bravely with a few pages of Plutarch's *Lives*, or some Gibbon, or *The Cloister and the Hearth;* I stick it for a while (two-thirds of the life of Benvenuto Cellini, three-quarters of *Moby Dick*, and those first two chapters of *A Tale of Two Cities*) and then I fall back into my old, slovenly, haphazard reading habits, going to the library every week or two and grabbing indiscriminately whatever books strike my fancy at the moment. This will never get me a place on a panel of literary experts, except as comic relief from excess erudition. I admire people who can chug unremittingly through the Great Books or read five pages of the encyclopedia every night. I just don't have the stamina and, besides, there's a certain intractability in me that balks at these practical, systematic, cold-blooded schemes. Despite the fact that I'm always consulting and constructing lists of books I ought to read, I don't really *want* to read books off a list—I want books to creep up on me unawares, like the time I was riding the subway in New York with a copy of Milton's *Areopagitica* (toward which I had only the shabbiest intentions) under my arm. I don't usually read in vehicles because it makes me queasy, but I started thumbing it anyway. I went three stations past my stop and had tears in my eyes.

I read: *Time, Mad, Redbook, Cosmopolitan, Maclean's* (a sort of Canadian *Saturday Evening Post*, you should forgive the expression), *Saturday Review*, the *Sunday New York Times*, and *Popular Science*. If I've read all those I read anything handy that's got words on it, like the backs of breakfast cereal packages and the labels on tin cans, and since Canada is a bilingual country I've learned a lot of French that way. If I ever go to France I'll get along fine in any situation that requires me to say FREE! INSIDE! or TAKE THIS COUPON TO YOUR GROCER! or TEAR BACK TO HERE or WRITE TODAY FOR YOUR FREE RECIPE BOOK! I can even ask *Vous avez essayé All-Bran?*

Maybe I'd better stay home.

When I read Beckett's *Waiting for Godot* all I could think of, all the way through, was The Emperor's New Clothes, The Emperor's New Clothes, The Emperor's New Clothes . . .

The sun is shining and Peter Cottontail is devouring incredible amounts of greenery gathered for him by the children in that first fine flush of pet-ownership. Everybody has a yo-yo and I have a small check for Norwegian rights to a story. I am continually puzzled about why Norwegian, Dutch, Danish, Finnish, Swedish, Australian, and South African women want to read my stories. It could be, of course, that they don't want to but simply have my stories foisted upon them by knuckle-headed editors; still, I prefer to think that somewhere in Oslo some nice, pretty, clever, amiable woman has just swept her kitchen floor, poured herself a cup of leftover coffee, and is reading one of my stories in a magazine and resting her feet. Hello there, Sigrid, I'm thinking of you.

April has the nicest name of all the months. It rhymes properly with nothing but itself and yet it is more poetic than June, which has a thick fistful of dull, thudding rhymes. April makes me tingle with expectation. April is full of love and impatience; can anyone ever really feel old in April?

Our wedding anniversary is in the middle of April, and next April, when I shall be thirty-eight years old, I shall have been married for half my life. Which is more than my husband will be able to say until 1964, such is the nature of mathematics. We skipped class one morning to get married—he was a senior and I a sophomore—and all in all it was a very ill-advised move, for we had only $45 a month between us and our prospects were, if not poor, precarious. We ate on 71 cents a day for the two of us, paid $15 a month for our room and kitchenette with a shared bath at the end of the hall, and squandered the remaining $8 on laundry, school supplies, and an occasional movie. We had a two-burner plate, a wobbly table, a squeaky, embarrassing bed, wallpaper with green ivy growing on an emphatic black trellis, and a view of a brick wall. When we wanted to know the weather, we had to put our heads out the window and look up. But after all, the weather didn't matter much to us.

Our landlady was a short, strong, tireless woman named Miss Sve. We have never forgotten her nor her name—nor the sight of her coming down the hall with a huge bureau balanced on her back—though I am sure she has long ago forgotten us. We were there only a short time. But husbands and wives of the ordinary sort don't often forget where they spent their honeymoon. We honeymooned at Miss Sve's rooming house.

Remembering Miss Sve and contemplating April, I can't help thinking more tolerantly of Virginia and Gordon and their plans. Gordon should have gotten into this book at least two months ago, but like a lot of other things he was left out. (Next time I write a book I'll be thoroughly organized and everything will be written down exactly where it belongs, although that does sound a little dull.) Gordon is, of course, Virginia's boy friend—in fact, he is her fiancé except when they quarrel and she gives him back his ring. Marriage is imminent and much-postponed, and nothing stands it its way but the slow grinding of the wheels at Children's Aid and a lot of dismal practical considerations. This, too, is an ill-advised marriage with precarious prospects. Dutifully I have discussed all these practical considerations with Virginia: the housing choice, between the Indian reserve and a city slum; the religious conflict, between Anglicanism and Catholicism; the threat of chronic unemployment for any young, unskilled Indian male; and the predictability of the unpredictable arrival of children. But Virginia is twenty and no longer, legally, a foster child (we call her our star boarder), even though she must get permission from the Children's Aid to marry; and she has been going with Gordon for over three years. Who wants to listen to advice in April? I didn't.

I like Gordon. He is shy and well-mannered, and when I compare him with the long-haired, tight-jeaned, sneering louts that infest our main street I decide that the world must be full of infinitely worse sons-in-law. Besides, in April eighteen years ago, *we* had known each other only a little over one year; a three-year courtship seems an eternity by comparison. Especially in April!

April is busy being bright and blowy instead of raining. Jill and two of her little friends are out with dolls and buggies. And I, after looking at the washing machine and deciding it would be easier to wash things out in the kitchen sink, have finally telephoned for a repairman. Wayne has been taking sheets and towels and the boys' jeans to the laundromat, but the suspense of wondering whether he will remember to pick them up on his way home is more than I can take. He is not exactly an absent-minded professor—Duncan will qualify for that title once he has his Ph. D.—but he has more to do than to remember to pick up laundry.

Polly is upstairs with the flu. Jill had it two days ago. Who will have it next?

I *know* who will have it last and worst. Miss Nightingale, that's who, having absorbed more than her share of contamination while doing her medical, motherly duty. I *always* have it last and worst.

Saturday night we went to see Alec Guinness in *The Horse's Mouth*. Now *there* is the kind of artist I would like to be: Jimson, I mean. I yearn to approach blank paper the way he approaches a blank wall. I kept thinking, mournfully, of The Book I Am Supposed to Be Writing. Oh, to be able to splash it on the paper with wild exuberance! Instead I dither and fume and fuss and pick and peck away, with all the wild exuberance of needlepoint. I can write letters exuberantly; in fact I am a tireless letter writer, to the dismay of all my exhausted correspondents who cannot possibly keep up with me. Some poor people get three letters for every one they manage to compose in reply, but I go merrily on because I simply enjoy it.

Why can't I write The Book I Am Supposed to Be Writing like that?

The sun beats down on the garden and we haven't done a thing with it. I'm sure Mr. D. has planted everything he intends to plant by now, and we haven't even begun.

I keep thinking of things I haven't put into this book, like the way Malcolm says "Oh, crumb!" every time I ask him to do something, and the way Duncan walks around, beside, behind, and in front of me while I work in the kitchen, discussing Plato and asking me what I know about

Sören Kierkegaard. (Nothing.) I could write a chapter on every room in this house, including the closets. I could write a chapter on each child and another one on the animals: Pepper the dog, Muff the cat, Sylvie the goldfish, Juliet the hamster, even Peter Cottontail the rabbit. When I'm sweeping and dusting around every morning I think of a hundred things I could write about, like the time Duncan started making fudge and somehow wound up with about two gallons of it, so that the house smelled like a chocolate factory and everybody's arm was worn out from beating. Or the time Malcolm took up taxidermy and tried to skin and stuff a field mouse we caught in the garden, executing it first in a neat homemade gas chamber constructed out of two jars, some glass tubing, and vinegar and baking soda. But if I put everything in that comes into my head, this would turn out to be quite a year, like the year 46 B.C. when Julius Caesar and Sosigenes the astronomer tidied up the sloppy calendar by throwing in three extra months, two of them between November and December (*that* would have been a good year for Christmas shopping if there had been any Christmas), and the whole thing worked out at 445 days. They called it the Year of Confusion, but for all the women who were twenty-nine years old in 46 B.C. it must have been a Year of Reprieve with all those extra days before they had to admit to being thirty. Why, if we had 445-day years, I'd only be thirty years old right now.

Come back, Little Caesar.

I must start dieting, or *I'll never lose those ten pounds.* I'll start by eschewing desserts.

Andy has decided he wants to get into Little League baseball. We are negative (being antiorganized-sport as far as children are concerned), but in this case permissive. I don't like baseball; we had to play it in high school and I hated to play with my glasses on but couldn't judge distances with them off. I always hid under the bleachers and waited for the whistle to call us back into the building. I liked *Damn Yankees*, though.

My husband also used to hide somewhere under the bleachers—not the same bleachers, not the same school—and play mumblety-peg and another jackknife game called Five Hundred with his friend Malcolm. He knows even less about baseball than I do. He probably hasn't even noticed that the Dodgers have moved to Los Angeles. He's further out of the main stream of American culture than I am; he doesn't even wash the car on Sundays.

Virginia tells me she and Gordon have set another date (they have been setting dates since Christmas), but I can tell you right now it's a very unrealistic one. It's only two weeks off, and I am dead certain that there won't be any permission from Children's Aid *that* soon. The only one of the practical considerations that seems to have been settled at last is the question of religion; they will be married in an Anglican ceremony. As far as all the rest is concerned—well, the Really Important Problems, I gather, are those involving a wedding gown and a pair of white shoes. Her sister Patsy's foster mother has already addressed invitations to a shower. Does Gordon need a black suit, Virginia asks me? What about his brother Melvin, as best man? And what color dress for Patsy, as bridesmaid?

I am, of course, absolutely useless in this crisis, never having had a shower or a wedding myself (my experience as a bride-in-ceremony lasted about 12 minutes flat in a courthouse, and I wore a plaid skirt and a white blouse and a pair of rather scuffed-up moccasins). But Patsy's foster-mother is one of those women who love weddings and I am happy to leave it all to someone who will do a good job of it. This provides a useful division of labor. While she worries about the wedding, I can worry about the marriage.

My advice to anyone planning marriage would be, *elope.*

It's April, however, and there's no sense trying to be reasonable. Eighteen years ago (when Virginia was two) *my* mother discussed all the practical considerations with me—and then let me make up my own mind.

The washing-machine repairman has come and gone. I was not wrong; it *was* the thing's lifeblood and now the top bearing is gone and the transmission is full of water and it would cost $40 to fix it. The repairman stood around in the kitchen while Wayne and I deliberated: $40 and still have to shove that machine back and forth; $40 and still have to wash frantically every weekend so the children will have school clothes to wear Monday morning; $40 and how much longer before the *next* $40? The repairman allowed it was a pretty poor prospect, and although I suspect he gets a bonus every time he talks somebody out of repairs and into a new appliance, he gave our machine such an eloquently contemptuous shrug that we surrendered on the spot. I have calculated that last year's bank loan—$500—must have only two months left before it's paid off, so we will touch our banker for a tidy thousand. With that much we can buy a washer *and* a drier (ha-ha, you old clothesline with northern exposure and two splices), pay for all the necessary electrical, gas, and plumbing work, and get a new, dogproof fence across the front of our property.

I am walking around in a state of shock, thinking of

merely setting dials and pushing buttons to do the laundry. Wayne has already taken down the hated ceiling drying rack and I have rolled the old machine out onto the back porch. The kitchen, large and old-fashioned anyway, looks cavernous. The electrician has estimated the cost of a new panel, new circuits, new wall outlets; the plumber will be around soon.

And another man we have already—the ice-cream man. Only mid-April and here he comes, tinkling "La donna e mobile," and we sing, "I am the ice-cream man, I take your dimes away, I make your teeth decay, Make money every day . . . I am the ice-cream man, I am the *ice*-cream man, I AM THE ICE-CREAM MAN and I'll soon-be-a-millionaire! With your dimes, with your dimes, I'll soon be a millionaire!" Despite this subtle propagandizing, the children come thundering in for dimes.

Mac and Duncan are working themselves to the bone for the school paper drive. Wayne drove them to school this morning with half a ton of it (I'm not just *saying* half a ton; I mean half a ton, duly weighed in lots on my bathroom scales), and somebody has promised them 800 pounds of *Christian Science Monitors* for tomorrow morning. The front porch is piled with papers and magazines to be bundled and tied, and Wayne and I keep finding things like *Sphere* or the *London Illustrated News* which we simply must filch for our own. In a fit of motherly foresight I went through a dozen copies of *McCall's* and abstracted all the pages with Betsy McCall paper dolls and put them away for (literally) a rainy day.

They are not slaving for mere glory; they inform us that there are eight or nine prizes to be awarded to those who bring in the most. The prizes range from a transistor radio down to a ball-point pen. They haven't decided how they'll divide this ball-point pen once they win it; a task for Solomon.

April makes me think of love and of tears, of lilacs and of death. *When lilacs last in the dooryard bloom'd, And the great star early droop'd in the western sky in the night, I mourn'd, and yet shall mourn with ever-returning spring.* Two deaths in the past can make me weep, two deaths of men I never knew. Lincoln's is one—April 14, 1865, almost a century ago. I have never really understood such sources of tears. Even as a child I wept for Abraham Lincoln, and perhaps it is as much the beautiful and tragic legend that calls up tears as it is the man, his life, his death. The other death, the other man, I knew nothing of as a child. February 17, 1600, Rome, a death by burning at the stake—the man, Giordano Bruno. I began to write a play about Bruno in cold blood, so to speak, but by the time I reached the end I wept over the lines I was writing and felt as close to him as if he had died but yesterday and in my own sight. He had looked at the infinite, incandescent stars and had supposed that other worlds were possible besides this one. But the earth, everyone knew, was the center of the universe, and man the center of God's attention, and the Church burned Bruno at the stake to demonstrate its infallibility. Why do I cry? Is it over the Giordano Bruno who died then, or the Bruno I re-created and became a part of?

I don't understand tears very well. They are hard to analyze, except chemically, and difficult to predict. One of my sisters cried when she first saw Crater Lake in Oregon. As for myself, the silver, blinding dome of Mt. Palomar Observatory left me unmoved, but when I entered the building and climbed the stairway and found myself standing outside the great glass panel and looking at the telescope itself, I had to turn my head away, and my throat began to ache. Lincoln and Bruno were noble men, and the telescope at Mt. Palomar is a noble instrument, so that I could imagine that I weep when confronted with nobility —if I didn't know better. Take the case of the merry-go-round, for example.

There's something about a merry-go-round I can't resist. It may be that wonderful, incomparable music that wheezes and grinds away and is usually just a tiny bit sour; or the dreamily plunging dappled horses and their bemused riders, half in a trance; or the swan, nearly as safe as solid ground, for the timid ones with sober, terrified faces. Whatever it is, I love merry-go-rounds, and now that I am past the riding age I am a merry-go-round watcher.

Being a merry-go-round watcher is an occupation at which I would be perfectly happy, except that I work at it under a terrible handicap. If you are ever watching a merry-go-round, look around for a moment and see if there is someone watching near you. If it is a nondescript brown-haired woman who keeps swallowing, seems to have a cold in her head, is clutching a soggy handkerchief, and looks at you with a hasty sidelong glance out of her watery eyes, just kindly, if you will, look the other way. It is probably me.

I don't know why merry-go-rounds make me cry. And if it were *just* merry-go-rounds, I could simply avoid them and be rid of the problem. But it isn't just merry-go-rounds, it's a whole long list of things. It's maudlin movies about aged schoolteachers. It's bagpipe music. It's flag-raising ceremonies and Boy Scout parades. It's magazine covers portraying first haircuts, family picnics, boys leaving for college. It's high school graduation. It's national anthems —any old national anthem, any old nation. It's the Christmas concert at the kindergarten, with the children banging rhythm sticks out of beat and singing "Jingle Bells" off key.

In my saner moments I'm as sentimental as a filing cabinet. I despise maudlin movies and really prefer something with all the pretty emotions of a Greek tragedy. I used to loathe most of my schoolteachers and if I didn't loathe them I held them in contempt. As for bagpipes, I am about 1/64th Scots, if any. I can cut hair without a qualm, no matter what the age of the child, and when I think of family picnics I think of making sandwiches by the bushel or sharing cold fried chicken with a horde of hungry yellow jackets. I am a washout as a patriot—scratch my patriotism and you'll find something close to anarchy—and besides, why should I be patriotic about somebody else's national anthem? But watch for me when the band strikes up; whether it's "The Marseillaise" or "Ja Vi Elsker Dette Landet," I'm blowing my nose and hoping nobody notices.

I'd like to know why I cry, why these appeals to sentimentality can be stronger than any logical, hard headed, rational thoughts I have on the matter. Am I, beneath the skin, just a sodden, susceptible, sniffling female? But the question that really bothers me is, what on earth am I supposed to do about it?

One always reads of people wiping away the unashamed, sentimental tear. But when I look around I never see anybody else wiping away the unashamed, sentimental tear. All I see is a collection of Great Stone Faces, dry-eyed and imperturbable. The only exception is in the dark of the movie theater, where some people come for the explicit (or illicit?) purpose of shedding tears and eating popcorn. But in the bright sunshine around the merry-go-round I am the only one who suffers from a summer cold-in-the-nose.

If it were only *una furtiva lagrima* I had to wipe away, I might get away with it unobserved. But it's generally a deluge, about as furtive as running up a red banner inscribed "I'm an Old Fool." For example, take that Christmas concert at the kindergarten. I made the mistake one year of going without a hanky, and I wound up sniffling like a marauding bear and sacrificing part of my own child's paper cutout of Santa Claus with whiskers of absorbent (thank heaven) cotton. I looked around at the rest of the mothers standing nearby. Maybe I just wasn't wearing my glasses, but it seemed to me they were all smiling happily; I couldn't see another damp eye in the place.

I don't know what I'm supposed to do; what is the proper etiquette for such occasions? Has Emily Post written on this subject? What does Mrs. Vanderbilt say? Are there rules? If it's really all right to give in and blow my nose and wipe my streaming eyes, then why am I so alone? What are the rest of you doing? Or am I the only one who cries at merry-go-rounds?

I also cry when a symphony orchestra tunes up (the most exciting music of all), and I cry whenever I hear an old, scratchy, worn-out children's record called "Little Indian Drum." I may have wept more tears, if one could measure them, over all these things than over any private sorrows.

Tears are a mystery.

Malcolm just came home sick. Whether it's flu or his report card I don't know, but the card is enough to make *me* sick. Andy, moreover, came home with a sore, swollen thumb, reported in at the doctor's office, and is now waiting for Wayne to pick him up there and take him to the hospital for an X-ray. There go his Little League plans. There, also, go any ideas I might have about serving dinner on time; X-rays at the general hospital take forever.

Meanwhile the porch groans under piles of newspaper and magazines and I feel as if the house must be gradually tilting in that direction; a few hundred pounds more and we'll suddenly be upended. The boys have turned in 3,000 pounds so far and now Duncan is stomping furiously about the house because Malcolm won't get up from his sickbed to help him bundle and tie for tomorrow's trip to school. I have put on the teakettle.

Tea—why, I hardly ever drank tea before coming to Canada. Nor ate "biscuits" imported from England and Scotland. Nor heard anyone say "vittamins," nor knew that movies are made out of fil-lum. Nor saw a Queen.

The Canadians need their Queen more than most of them realize. If they lost their Queen they could be thrown off balance in their perpetual struggle to remain Canadian. To be Canadian means to be more British than the Americans and more American than the British. This is a difficult position to maintain—without a Queen, impossible.

If you do not dress like a Californian, act like a Texan, and talk as if you came from Brooklyn, no Canadian will believe you are from south of the border.

Canada has no national flag and nobody knows whether the national anthem is "God Save the Queen," "The Maple Leaf Forever," or "O Canada." All three of these, however, are more singable than "The Star-Spangled Banner." I have never decided whether I get a lump in my throat from "The Star-Spangled Banner" out of patriotic sentiment or soprano's laryngitis.

In Canada Thanksgiving comes before Halloween, Halloween is the time for fireworks, and nobody pays any attention to July 1, which is the Canadian version of the Fourth of July. It celebrates the coming into force of the

British North America Act passed by the British Parliament —a kind of absentee birth of the Canadian nation—and seems to be about as interesting to Canadians as are the present-day activities of the British Parliament; that is, only the Canadian Broadcasting Corporation and the artists who draw the cover illustrations for *Maclean's* take much notice of it.

Canadian patriots and the CBC tried to replace Davy Crockett and the American West with Pierre Radisson and the Canadian North. They couldn't.

It's amazing what they learn in school these days. Duncan's science book has a marvelous diagram which explains perfectly the inner workings of a toilet flush box. Now if sombody could just drum into these boys' heads that they ought to lift the seat first . . .

There is absolutely no point in trying to stay on a diet when I ask the children what they want for dessert and they say ice cream with chocolate sauce. What I really need is a recipe for a dessert that the children would love and I would detest, perhaps something made out of marshmallows, peanut butter, and bubble gum.

This diet business is depressing. Why, every month in the women's magazines there are women who have lost forty, fifty, ninety, even a hundred pounds and more; and I can't get rid of *ten.* Women are improving themselves in every way in those magazines; I see articles all the time about how some dowdy little frump was changed (usually with the help of the magazine's beauty staff) into a charming creature. Despite the fact that the frump looked like an individual and the charming creature looks like all other charming creatures (basic black, string of pearls, no tummy at all, and her feet neatly arranged to form an 87° angle), I am intrigued at the thought of being magically transformed.

I have from time to time laid careful plans for such a magical transformation. They begin with dieting and a schedule that calls for daily exercise, facials, manicures, a new coiffure, one hundred strokes with the hairbrush every night, etc. They end practically where they begin, too, because I am not only a hungry woman, I am a lazy one besides. The way I get a manicure, for example, is to sit and stare at my fingernails while trying to think of the next word at the typewriter. Usually I discover one fingernail is broken or else one has grown inexplicably longer than the other nine, and I hunt around in my desk drawer for a pair of scissors to even the score. I use nail polish to mark names on the tin cans the children use for piggy banks.

As for my hair, I chop off a bit in front now and then, and wear the rest of it twisted up and skewered to my head at the back. Sometimes after I wash it I get daring and pour on half a bottle of Brown Panther or Red Cheetah, but my hair is more stubborn than the hair of women in the ads; it stays the same old hair-colored hair. No wonder only my hairdresser (me) knows for sure.

Exercise, however, is something I really ought to try again. I tried it once, when I faithfully struggled through the entire course of a beauty school by correspondence. I beat myself to a pulp in the shower every day, lived on oranges and raw carrots, and had a dozen little pots and jars of fascinating greases and oils to smear on my face. I sat on the floor and banged my behind methodically until I felt as if I'd been caught stealing cookies. I lay with my head down and my feet up until I was pixillated. I don't know if I was any more beautiful when I was through, but I can tell you I was a darned sight more tired.

I suppose I could take up bowling, or borrow one of the boys' bikes and take a brisk five-mile ride before breakfast every day, or learn to leap out of bed and touch my toes twenty times before getting dressed. But there's no sense deluding myself; I have a hard enough time merely getting out of bed and filling the coffee pot. That's exercise enough for before breakfast, and I get the rest of my day's quota fishing for wadded-up socks under the beds, groping for the soap that fell behind the bathtub, relighting the oven pilot light, and running up and down stairs carrying trays to sick children. Actually, if I had the life of leisure I am (as a Modern Housewife) rumored to have, I would probably weigh about 250 pounds.

Nobody has yet invented a laborsaving device for picking up after kids.

And who wants to be charming anyway? I haven't got time to stand around all day with my feet at an 87° angle.

Our big cherry is sifting a snow of blossoms on the grass, and the transparent apple next to it is trembling on the edge of bloom. All the gardens for blocks around are burning with tulips and azaleas. Our lilac may bloom any day now. Only fools would complain of our northwest rain; the trees back east don't even have leaves yet. I see by the World Almanac that there's twice as much precipitation in Mobile, Alabama, as there is here. I know it's impossible, but it's right there in black and white.

I should have some system, like a series of dots . . . . . or maybe * * * * * to indicate the passage of time. Perhaps something on the order of $%&')*!&"@¢! would be most suitable at the moment. Anyway, I've lost three pounds, and for the benefit of those who would like to try my system, here's how I did it. I got The Blight.

Wednesday night: Andy's thumb wasn't broken, just sprained. We had a fashionably late dinner, but Mac chose to lie unfashionably on his bed upstairs, retching into a plastic bucket.

Thursday morning: I had breakfast. This proved to be a mistake, and I spent the rest of the day on *my* bed, sipping at a glass of water.

Friday morning: Wayne had to fly to Portland at 5 A.M. to give a talk to some group or other. I got up and promptly fell flat again. Virginia stayed home from work long enough to get the kids off to school, and then left me with Jill. Rising to the occasion, Jill tiptoed about being angelic and playing a silent and solitary game with her dolls. When lunchtime arrived, I could hear the refrigerator door opening and shutting, and she said something about cottage cheese but I didn't inquire too closely, deciding to trust her judgment as a dietician even if she isn't four years old yet. After lunch she went out to feed Peter Cottontail, came back to announce (in a whisper) that he was "playing dead." I crept out of bed and went to investigate. He wasn't playing dead, he *was* dead. There was nothing to do but leave him there until the boys got home and could hold a funeral. Virginia brought Gordon home and they made supper for the children. I lay on my bed under a smog of hamburger and toyed with a cup of bouillon.

Saturday morning: I got up, made oatmeal, ate two spoonfuls, staggered back to bed. By afternoon, however, I was able to stay upright, although the floor had a tendency to be somewhere else every time I put my foot on it. Jelly-kneed, I wobbled downstairs to admire my new appliances in the basement; not hooked up yet, but looking fine.

By Sunday night I was almost human again and ready for almost anything except for Wayne to come in cheerily from his trip and tell me that he had been approached about a new job and we might be moving in the fall.

It's only might and a very small might at that, but I've been going around the house with a lump in my throat and the wastebasket is full of soggy wept-into Kleenex.

There's nothing so special about this house except I love it. It isn't a magnificant showplace, we didn't build it ourselves, and it's not particularly weird, wonderful, and eccentric. I thought, when I began this book, that it might be kind of a disappointment to the reader to find out that we don't live in a broken-down mansion with twenty rooms, turrets, winding staircases, and an erratic dumb-waiter one of the children might get stuck in. This is only an undistinguished house of no particular style at all, an old, green-shingled house with a red roof and a large, somewhat drooping porch running across the front of it. But there is stained glass at the tops of some of the windows, and the afternoon light pours in like golden syrup. The big old dogwood tree nearly scrapes the windowpanes in the kitchen nook, and the living-room ceiling has white beams crossing a field of Chinese red. The floors all slant, one way or another; upstairs, the middle bedroom has a gentle, noticeable curve where it projects out over the front porch. It is a dusty house, full of ledges and bitty corners and plate rails. It has acres of painted wood paneling and the front hall, stairway, and upstairs hall are all painted white, the better to see small dirty fingerprints by. But a woman came by not long ago, knocking on my door. "I'm house hunting," she said, "and I want to find a big old house like this. You wouldn't be thinking of selling, would you?" "Oh, no," I said. She fidgeted a moment. "Please forgive me," she said, "but would you mind if I just stepped in and looked?" I didn't mind, and she walked into the living room. "Oh dear," she cried, with a sob of envy in her voice, "this is just the kind of house I want!"

This house wasn't engineered for family living. It probably wasn't even designed by a bona fide architect. It was just built by somebody who wanted to build a house.

Down in the basement, as I write, the plumber and the gaspipe fitter are pounding and banging and scraping away at who knows how many $$ an hour. Tomorrow I will be able to do laundry, but my joy is tempered.

I have a confession to make. I could leave what friends I have behind without too many heartaches, for you can keep friends no matter how many miles intervene, but when I thought of our family doctor, I broke down and ran for the Kleenex again. Good family doctors, like good family houses, are hard to come by.

Sniff. I'll blow my nose and take a firm grip on myself. This prospective job may never materialize at all, and even if it does it may not be good enough to take.

Whoever called them laborsaving devices has never seen a woman with a new washer and drier. I am positively exhausted from running all over the house to find everything that can possibly be washed in the washer, carting it downstairs, washing it, drying it, and carting it all back to be put away. It would be a simpler business if I didn't have to rush down to see what the machines are doing every time I hear one of them make a new noise I can't identify. I don't know whether I expect them to blow up or overflow or exactly *what*, but I have never been entirely en rapport with machinery of any description. In fact I have a monumental lack of faith that is positively un-American. I may have been born in the wrong century or at any rate the wrong country, because I think I was intended to do my laundry down at the river by the stone-pounding method.

I didn't even like trading in my old treadle sewing machine for a new electric portable. The man who took it away said it was going to an overseas missionary society, so I hope some happy housewife in her native village is sitting there and treadling away, running up a hem on her Sunday dress. Hello there, Nkaina, I'm thinking of you.

April draws to a close. Polly is cutting out paper dolls, Cam is playing some elaborate make-believe with Jill, Andy has gone to the Y with a friend, Mac is attending first-aid class at St. John's Ambulance Corps, and Duncan has just come in after stopping by the lumber yard to ask them to phone me with a cost estimate on 60 feet of fencing across the front of our lot. Wayne has bought pansies, petunias, and snapdragons to set out in the garden. Virginia and Gordon have had to postpone the wedding date again, but even official red tape must come to an end sometime, and May looks like a sure thing. Our rhubarb by the back fence is high and bright and delicious.

We had some students over the other night and allowed our offspring to join the party. This may have been a dreadful mistake, however, as it refired one young married student's ambition to have twelve children (his wife swears she's already exhausted with two). He went on a tour of the upper regions and was delighted with the miser's hoard of radio parts, the hamster, the cases of rocks and fossils, the general confusion (his wife said she didn't dare look, she wasn't up to it).

I see among Duncan's library books that he is reading *A New Approach to Schizophrenia*. But he still whines if the Raisin-Bran is all gone when he gets to the breakfast table.

MAY

WHATEVER happened to May Day? When I was a runny-nosed, freckle-faced schoolgirl, we always spent the last week of April making small colored-paper baskets, and early on the morning of May 1 we filled them with flowers and tiptoed around the neighborhood, hanging them on doorknobs. I haven't found a basket on *my* doorknob since I grew up. All the gentler aspects of May Day seem to have vanished. When May Day rolls around now I think of (1) a distress call, *May Day! May Day!* and Steve Canyon is in trouble somewhere, or (2) battalions of workers marching across Red Square.

I'm not anti-labor. Who, me?—the daughter of a Wobbly? When I was five I could recite "The working class and the employing class have nothing in common . . ." and sing "Arise, ye prisoners of starvation, Arise, ye wretched of the earth!" or that stirring chorus from *The Preacher and the Slave*, "You will eat, bye and bye, In that glorious land above the sky; Work and pray, live on hay, You'll get pie in the sky when you die!"

No, I'm not anti-labor, I'm just pro-flower. I wish somebody would bring back those May Baskets, that's all.

Our garden is loveliest in May. Later, in midsummer, it becomes more lush, with beans festooning the palisade of beanpoles that outlines our free-form corn patch (trust *us* to have a free-form corn patch) and the squash vines growing wildly everywhere, even through the back fence and into our neighbor's garden. But in May it is lovelier. The azaleas are still there and the rhododendrons join them with creamy white, pearly pink, and a fiery magenta. The giant dogwood outside the kitchen nook is loaded with white, velvety flowers, and the one west of the house keeps putting its branches into Malcolm's bedroom window and shedding petals on the floor. Out in front the hawthorn droops clusters of vivid pink. The tulips are almost gone, but a few lavender ones remain, the hardiest of the lot. There are pansies and lily-of-the-valley, bleeding-heart, a few leftover hyacinths, and all kinds of little white flowers I have never learned to identify.

It's not a tidy, well-cared-for, manicured garden. It's a mess, really, with a jungly profusion of weeds. The grass is half plantain, the rose bed is half chickweed, but the weeds are not the worst of it. Our garden, like our house, is lived in—and it looks it. The children leave their bicycles and stilts lying around and there's a trail of paper wrappers and small sticks, mute evidence that once again the ice-cream man stopped outside our driveway and all the children repaired to our yard to eat. Old mashed cardboard cartons, discarded from bicycle carriers, are not as pretty as peonies; and that dainty, lacy thing I spy in the shrubbery is not a new blossom but a broken badminton shuttlecock.

We need a Japanese gardener, or several of them. We also need a little man with one of those pointed sticks and a gunny sack. Nevertheless, I love our garden. Even in the rain—and it is raining now as I write this and the rain is pounding on the top of the garden table which we just today moved out of a corner of the living room into the garden (which is why it is raining, I suppose)—it is a very nice garden. It has, like Herrick's lady, "a sweet disorder," with its lawn certainly in a fine distraction, a hedge neglectful, a tempestuous flower bed, a careless rockery. Yes, these "Do more bewitch me than when art Is too precise in every part." We are planning a new fence because we must, but I'll hate to see the old one go. It is a lovable fence, all gray and falling down, propped up with braces—a perfect fence for roses and hollyhocks and foxglove and mint to grow against, and I won't like a new fence half so much, all tan and naked-looking. There are just some things I like old: fences, barns, trees, and houses.

I take no credit whatsoever for our garden. You've heard of a green thumb? I have a neighbor who raises African violets. She has lots of them, and by lots of them I mean windows ranged with shelves and shelves of them and half the basement taken up with tables groaning under them, and all thriving in an overpowering fashion. This woman has a real green thumb.

I have, on the other hand, what is called a *brown thumb.* I can grow old carrot tops in a saucer—sometimes. But to bring an African violet into our house is to sentence it to death. First I desiccate it with cheerful neglect; then I drown it with guilt and remorse.

It isn't only indoor plants. Despite my love for them, I simply can't raise flowers. If there are flowers in our garden, they were either there when we moved in or else my husband put them there. I don't really know them from the weeds until they bloom; then, of course, I'm all admiration. All *I* seem to be able to raise are radishes and beets and chard and lettuce. I know a radish when I see one, and I can tell a beet plant when it is only ⅛ of an inch out of the ground. I suppose this means that my gastric faculties are harder at work than my aesthetic faculties. I don't know. But it would explain why I do fairly well with a dish of carrot tops.

Actually, my greatest indoor gardening successes have not been exactly horticultural. The thing I grow best is what we used to call a "Depression Garden"—the kind you make by putting lumps of coal or pieces of brick in the bottom of a dish and pouring over it a combination of bluing, ammonia, and a few drops of iodine. I'm a whiz at that sort of thing. It doesn't need to be watered.

The boys did win the ball-point pen—and they've lost it already.

And I—I've gotten back what *I* lost: those three pounds.

There is no news whatsoever about Wayne's possible new job.

I have dumped everything out of my winter purse (black) and put it all into my summer purse (white). I have two, and two only, because I hate the things. I envy men their multitudinous, omnipresent pockets. I have never had a handbag that matched a pair of shoes, nor a hat that matched either. I have two hats—in a box, on a shelf. They stay there, year in and year out. Once in a while I take the box down and dust it off and then put it back. Sometimes I even open the box, take out the hats, try them on, look in the mirror, wince, put them back in the box, and put the box back on the shelf.

The kitchen, minus the old washing machine, has been rearranged so that Wayne and I can eat in the nook again; I'm just close enough to the children's table to leap up 1½ seconds too late to grab bottles of milk as they get knocked over. But the nice thing is that we can bird-watch as we eat now, and we have our field guide to western birds lying handy on the windowsill so we can consult over what variety of finch is sitting on the gooseberry bush or what just flew into the laurel hedge. We are, anyway, great looker-uppers. *Bring the encyclopedia!* I cry. *Get the dictionary! Where's Fowler? Who has the World Almanac? What happened to the big green atlas?* I would like very much to report that this has resulted in a family of brilliant students, but I can't. It isn't modesty that forbids me, it's honesty. Take Malcolm, for example. On our family trip to Baja California he kept one sharp eye out the car window and the other glued to the guidebooks (*Western Birds, Mammals, Rocks and Minerals*), and he read all the labels in every museum, aquarium, and zoo from here to San Diego and back again. But Mac has passed six times into the next grade by the skin of his teeth, and none of the passionate enthusiasm he displays for knowledge at home survives that morning journey up the front steps of the school building. It is quite possible, you see, to do all the right things at home to instill that thirst for learning—and still get all the wrong results on the report card. Mac, armed with a guidebook and stalking something through the bushes, leaping from rock to rock, or even rushing from one glass case to another in a museum, is *not* Mac incarcerated, squirming, at a desk in the schoolroom.

A paternal Ph.D. and a maternal Phi Beta Kappa key do not automatically produce six intellectual giants for offspring, even in an atmosphere heavy-laden with the printed word. The children of Democrats are sometimes unaccountably Republicans, and ministers' wives may even give birth to atheists. The hardest thing parents have to learn to do is to keep their hands off their children's lives. If there is any virtue in having six children in this overpopulated world, it's that they outnumber you and divide your attention.

Of course this is all fairly easy to say when my children want to be a physicist, an airplane designer, a naturalist, a geographer (that's Cam and I hope his subject matter is still here for him when the time comes), a ballet dancer, and a little girl four years old (Jill can't see very far ahead yet). I might not be so unconcerned if they wanted to be rock-and-roll singers or masters of ceremony on television quiz shows.

Duncan has just come downstairs: *clomp, stomp, clomp, stomp!* "Did you get 'em all? Are they all dead?" I ask. "What? Who?" he wants to know, falling for it again. "The bugs under the stair carpet. I thought you were trying to kill them." But Duncan at least walks down, step by step; the others ski down, removing a little more carpet each time.

In May I always get an attack of wanderlust, and in May we always begin making optimistic plans for the summer. The research my husband will finally write up, now that he is free from classes! The things we will do to the garden! The stories I will finish! The camping trips! We will eat out in the back yard more often. We will build a barbecue pit. I will get a sun tan. We will certainly not let those long, golden, lovely summer days just dribble away between our fingers—not *this* summer. We swear each summer is going to be different from the last. We're very sure of this in May and we can even hold fast to our belief all the way to the second week in August.

But it is May and the corn has been planted and our property-tax assessment turned out to be smaller than I expected after all the scare headlines in the papers. Cameron, a full-fledged Junior Forest Warden, is walking around in a blinding red shirt several sizes too large for him but the smallest size the uniform comes in; and Malcolm is still attending a first-aid course every Saturday morning at St. John's Ambulance, working doggedly for more badges for me to sew on his sleeve. Andy is planning a square-dance party for some of his sixth-grade friends. Virginia and Gordon will get married on the 16th at St. James's Anglican Church, and Virginia is floating around two feet off the ground, barely communicating with us earth-bound humans. Wayne is grading final examinations for Anthropology 200, the introductory course.

May is also the time I feel like stripping down the house for clean, uncluttered living, and I have been going through the drawers and closets in an ecstatic fury, filling cardboard cartons for the Salvation Army. I love throwing things out, especially clothes, and it's a good thing I do, because everybody else around here loves saving things: one thrower-outer ranged against all these savers has really got to have guts. I have filled up four cardboard cartons already and (brutally) shoved into one of them Wayne's ancient tatterdemalion Navy trenchcoat ("But it has a real leather lining!" he cried, trying not to see the various rips, tears, mends, worn spots, cuffs innocent of any fabric at all, and a general fringed appearance) on the supposition that next fall we will somehow or other scrape up the wherewithal for a new one.

The boys' clothes, naturally, are handed down as long as they will hold together, and Polly's clothes go to Jill. But since the boys all have abrasive knees and knifelike elbows, the only garments that reach the end of the line (Cameron, age nine) are short-sleeved shirts and long-sleeved shirts that have been converted into short-sleeved shirts. He has about two dozen of these and some of them never get worn at all unless I turn the contents of his shirt drawer upside down.

I love hand-me-downs. I even wear them myself; my mother-in-law is just the right size to discard garments in my direction. I have her old blue jeans on right now.

It dawns on me that I am going to have to wear a hat to Virginia's wedding!

One of my sisters writes that she gave a party for eighty-four people the other day. Suddenly the misanthrope in me comes to the fore; I am trying hard to think of eighty-four people I'd want in my house at once, and I can't think of eighty-four people I'd want *anywhere.* I don't really dislike people. It's just that large groups of them somehow anesthetize me. A glaze comes over my eyes and a sort of buzz or hum sounds in my ears, effectively cutting out the names of all the people I'm introduced to. Five minutes after the introductions, when people are moving around the room and getting separated from their spouses, Dr. Buzz (or is it Mr. Hum?) squirms past me, sloshing tea into my saucer, and inquires brightly whether I know where his wife has got to. I crane my neck and look helpfully about, knowing full well that I've no idea whether the woman in the purple hat was Mrs. Buzz and the one in the tight pea-green dress was Mrs. Hum, or vice versa. "No, I don't see her," I say, but he has already gone with a glad cry and is moving toward the exit, towing behind him a woman with little beady-eyed furs and crooked seams. I don't remember *her* at all.

It's a good thing my husband isn't a politician.

Andy's party is in progress down in the rec room. It is strictly Andy's party, and the other boys are wandering around the house complaining bitterly of the noise, their noses out of joint. "Can't you tell them to be *quiet?*" Malcolm storms; he really feels left out. "*Girls,*" Duncan sneers. ("Well," says Andy, "you've got to get interested in girls *sometime!*" But I think Duncan has sworn to get his Ph.D. first and *then* get interested in girls.) Cameron reports that the lights are out and they're playing Spin the Bottle—with kissing! But it is only Saturday afternoon and I see by the clock that they will have to break up and go home in half an hour or so; there are still mothers who guard their nubile daughters with old-fashioned zeal, and nighttime parties are forbidden, and for this I am grateful. (Polly has just gone down to snoop and has been ejected violently; she is weeping. First I console her, then I scold her for snooping, then I must collar Andy and scold *him* for being rude.) They aren't square-dancing, incidentally. Nobody had any square-dance records and nobody tried very hard to find any either. It could be that they never had much intention of square-dancing (oh, cynic!) but simply knew the obvious: if you say "square-dance party" you get a quicker parental yes than if you say "rock-and-roll party." The hideous and monotonous throbbing pulsating up from the rec room indicates that it wasn't too difficult to locate a large supply of rock-and-roll records.

Andy is on the way to becoming a teen-ager; Malcolm, perhaps. Cameron is too young yet. But Duncan, the oldest, already thirteen, is not a teen-ager; he is an old-fashioned *adolescent*. There was a difference even when I was a schoolgirl; some of us danced the Lambeth Walk and the Big Apple, and had dates with boys, and even went steady (though there were fewer steadies then than there are now); and then there were some of us who wrote poetry and brooded and had undying secret passions for aloof members of the opposite sex and went to the movies in safe unmixed parties. Duncan is moody, broody, and full of *Schmerz*, and on his thirteenth birthday a cloud of worries seemed to condense over his head. Some of this is probably glandular in origin, a sort of free-floating anxiety that attaches itself to whatever is at hand.

In the midst of one of his blackest moments I attempted some feeble-minded psychology and told him to go upstairs and *write down* everything that was bothering him. He came back with a list: "I worry about (1) not being a success in life, (2) about schoolwork, (3) about not having enough money, (4) about not being able to do the things I want at the moment, (5) ABOUT EVERYTHING I ATTEMPT TO DO." Pretty all-inclusive. Worries (3) and (4) are, essentially, the same thing, and there's nothing to be done about it, short of starting over again with another paper route. We had two years of that, and while Duncan gloried in his purchases—a new bicycle, a 35-mm camera, chemistry equipment—we suffered as a family from the nervous strain of finding someone to do the route whenever we wanted to go somewhere for a day or two. (Of course they're right about a newspaper route building character. When the snow is a foot deep and the boy can't use his bicycle and nobody wants to go out and help deliver the papers on foot, it can't help but build character to get out there and *do the job.* Of course, I did look a little silly trudging along in the snow with a shopping bag full of evening papers, but it built character, and I'm a better woman for it.)

Worrying about schoolwork seems a little strange for a boy who stands seventh in the entire grade, but Duncan has grown to dislike certain subjects and has figured out sly ways of "getting by" and avoiding work. I suspect his conscience is bothering him. What (1) is I'm not quite sure, but I think it is related to the fact that he is already thirteen years old and hasn't gotten on the track of a Scientific Discovery yet. As for (5), it comes and goes, and he swings wildly and unpredictably between "I can do anything" and "Everything I do is a failure," between arrogance and tearful misery. And—if this weren't enough! —Jill has for some unknown reason taken to tormenting him; she can propel him into a state of complete disintegration by walking up to him, looking at him insolently, and saying, "I don't like you any more, Duncan!"

My income-tax refund has come in the mail. The amount is substantial (what uncalled-for optimism drove me to keep on making those quarterly installment payments when I wasn't earning anything?), and I have been entertaining an estimate man who has been thumping posts in the basement and measuring that part of the floor where the old furnace and coalbin used to be. We are going to have six posts replaced and concrete poured. I have also been studying a leaflet on fences.

But oh, to be less practical! I have been dreaming the past couple of days over a brochure on my desk, a huge envelope, 10 x 13 inches, crammed with booklets, application forms, and a Talent Test. *Art School for Every-*

one—Everywhere. If we didn't need a fence, if we didn't need something over that bare, exposed dirt in the basement, if those posts that hold the house up were just a little more solid . . . I've even gone so far as to take a pencil to the Talent Test, and I've drawn a barn and a silo and some silky hair on a cocker spaniel.

But something holds me back. Something besides the fee, I mean.

When I was a young girl people used to tell me all the time that I was artistic. What they really meant, I think, was that I loved to mess around with colored pencils and pastel sticks and jars of poster paints. I always made my own Christmas cards, for example; and I also made horrid little cutout silhouettes which I mounted on the backs of dime-store purse mirrors with the silver scraped off. I think I sold these to less discriminating schoolmates who thought they were pretty. I spent a lot of time creating various artistic monstrosities, and was not particularly daunted by the fact that when I got into an honest-to-goodness art class in ninth grade the teacher evinced no interest in my talent whatsoever. It seemed inconceivable that my unquenchable enthusiasm could exist without some spark of genius to make it worth while.

I went on drawing and painting through high school and college. Then I went to New York for graduate work in sociology, and because my classes were in the evening, I enrolled in art school in the daytime. I bought oils and a palette and brushes, and I started in a life class under a well-known American painter. The boy whose easel stood next to mine paid no attention to the model; he was painting a series of tortured faces in nightmare colors. The boy whose easel was in front of mine also paid no attention to the model; he was painting what looked like old kitchen linoleum in various shades of brown mud. But the model was there, shivering slightly, for my convenience, and I began to paint her. I had no experience with oil paints; I hadn't a clue to go on. And the well-known American painter had the habit of walking past me as if I were invisible. I painted laboriously, meticulously, and after I had suffered unnoticed for five weeks, the well-known painter finally stopped by my easel and looked at my painting for several minutes of thoughtful silence. "Mn-hm," he said, speaking his first (and last) words to me, "a very interesting primitive."

I knew what a primitive was, and if I was going to be a self-taught artist, why was I wasting my money on the well-known painter? I did one other oil painting, a lurid portrait of a young Negro writer of my acquaintance, a work which was a stunningly accurate likeness and a perfectly dreadful oil painting. I went away from art school beaten and miserable; I was talentless, I had deluded myself all these years, I could never be an artist.

But there was a kind of vindication waiting for me, a single moment of glory. I still carried a sketchbook around, and I had it with me one night when I was eating dinner in a small Greenwich Village café. We ate there because some of my friends knew the proprietors and could occasionally get a meal on the cuff. It was a place of great local color—candles flickered on wobbly tables, someone drummed, a West Indian dancer danced, and I sat and idly sketched a portrait of a young woman at the next table. When I was through, her husband, who had been watching me, got up and came over to my table.

"Why, it's very good," he said, almost shyly.

I tore it out of the sketchbook and handed it to him, and he smiled down at it. "How much?" he asked.

Suddenly I saw myself as he saw me—a bohemian, a Village character, a romantic figure in his tourist's dream.

A great feeling of well-being settled over me and with great nonchalance I said, "One dollar."

He gave it to me and I folded it and put it in my wallet, smiling inscrutably.

And now, it doesn't really matter that when Jill comes to me with a crayon and a scrap of paper and says, "Draw me a cat, Mommy," I draw a little whiskered circle on a big circle, two triangle ears, and a scimitar tail. I was once, for a moment, akin to Toulouse-Lautrec. I was, when I took that dollar in my hand, an Artist.

The sketchbooks lie at the bottom of a drawer somewhere, and the hideous likeness of the young man (who is now, in his mid-thirties, a distinguished figure in the literary world) is stowed away in the linen cupboard in the upstairs hall. Perhaps I had best put the brochure and the Talent Test back in the envelope and stow them somewhere, too, and leave well enough alone.

If I want to paint, there is always the downstairs bathroom; it's a rather grisly shade of pink.

I haven't figured out yet whether the new laundry equipment is really saving me fabulous amounts of time or simply enabling me to do a lot more laundry.

The garden is full of little green and yellow warblers. If I do save any time on the laundry, I spend it sitting at the table after breakfast, lingering there to watch the birds. That isn't what I intended to save time *for*, but it's nice anyway.

I have just been standing in the doorway of Virginia's room, looking at the nest from which the bird has flown, a nest strewn with shoes, sweaters, souvenirs, snapshots, bobby pins, and a pink crinoline standing by itself in a corner. I can remember, just a year ago, when the room's décor still included a wall papered with movie stars: Doris Day, Rock Hudson, Jimmy Dean; but as the girl grew up, the pictures came down, and the movie magazines and *True Confessions* lay on a shelf, gathering dust, nearly forgotten by a young woman who had learned to read books.

I didn't cry at the wedding. Maybe I was afraid that an unexpected sob might pop a button from my old blue faille sheath into which I had mercilessly stuffed myself, or that if I reached up to wipe away that unashamed, sentimental tear I might knock askew that unaccustomed hat. Our children—the boys looking strange and stiff in sport coats and slacks, the girls with white velvet bandeaux and daisies on their heads—had never been inside a church before, unless you count our visit to the Mission San Juan Capistrano, but they betrayed no unfamiliarity other than Jill's sotto voce question before the ceremony, "Mommy, why is the building all decorated up?" Melvin was an exemplary best man, Patsy wore yellow, and Virginia's father had come to town in time to give the bride away. The bride's bouquet and the groom's voice were both unsteady, but the ceremony was mercifully brief and in scant minutes we were threading our way through traffic to a small reception. It was there that emotion caught up with me, when Virginia's father shook our hands and thanked us for finishing the job of raising his eldest daughter. I think I know what it might be like to swallow a golf ball without a chaser.

Still, I know in my heart that the compliment and the gratitude are mainly undeserved; we worked no miracles and did nothing great and generous. We simply moved over a bit and made room, and if we displayed any particular virtues in this matter of being foster parents, they were only patience and tolerance—the same virtues we need for our own children, anyway, and for *them* sometimes in backbreaking quantities.

Why must organizations like Children's Aid Society search so desperately for foster parents while at the same time long lists of people wait endlessly and hopelessly to adopt children? There must be hundreds, no, thousands of children who cannot be adopted but whose parents will never be able to come to claim them and give them the home they need. And even at that risk—why, when you love your own child, you have no guarantee that he will be there to love tomorrow.

Duncan is supposed to memorize ten lines of poetry for English class; he took my copy of Untermeyer's *Great Poems* to school with him and chose his selection during study hour. By nightfall he was wrestling furiously with it, mumbling and muttering, and I finally asked him what it was. He had chosen ten lines of Walt Whitman's, and perhaps ten of the most impossible-to-memorize lines he could have found, devoid of any of the aspects of poetry that make it adhere to the mind and tongue. He didn't want to give up, but after another hour's application had produced no results, he finally decided to choose another one. I thumbed through the book and suggested James Elroy Flecker's "To a Poet a Thousand Years Hence," which I read aloud to him—causing me to burst promptly into tears. I am just like one of Pavlov's dogs salivating at the sound of the bell; it doesn't matter how many times I read that poem, I *always* cry. "*I who am dead a thousand years, And wrote this sweet archaic song* . . ." Already my throat begins to ache, and by the time I reach, "*O friend unseen, unborn, unknown, Student of our sweet English tongue,*" I'm blinking and biting my lip and hunting for the handkerchief I need when I finish, "*Since I can never see your face, And never shake you by the hand, I send my soul through time and space To greet you. You will understand.*" Look it up—it's a lovely, lovely poem.

The old house is groaning and complaining rheumatically as the men in the basement jack her up for the new posts. There's no question of correcting all her sag; they've raised her an inch and if they do any more there won't be a door in the house that will open and shut. Even now I find myself holding my breath and expecting the whole works to crumble into a heap of lumber and plaster. In fact, I don't know why this hasn't happened before. When the workmen called me down to see one of the old posts in cross section, I flicked it with a fingernail and the wood dust fell away in showers. We might just as well have had columns of cotton batting holding us up all this time. It wasn't the posts, obviously; it was probably something intangible, like strength of character.

While they hammer and saw and make alarming noises in the basement, I have been painting. Not oil portraits—walls. We have begun, with unseemly and indecent haste, to redecorate Virginia's room so that Wayne can use it for a study. Togetherness is something that simply cannot be indulged simultaneously with the pursuit of scholarly research, and the incessant clatter of my typewriter seems to interfere with his investigation of the intricacies of Indian social and economic organization or the complexities of Salish grammar. I am painting the room a pale green.

However, I am one of those people who should never be allowed to get near paint and a paintbrush. There are people like that; my uncle John was one. Once he had occasion to paint something orange. I don't know now what it was, but I do know that before Uncle John finished he had painted the wastebaskets, dustpans, stepladder, stools—even the wooden handles of a couple of kitchen carving knives were orange. Orange is a dandy color for pumpkins, oranges, and interurban trains, but I was glad when he ran out of paint. Well, yesterday I painted for a while and then came in here to the kitchen nook to write. I wrote a bit, but the smell of paint and turpentine was in my nostrils; my senses were inflamed, you might say, and I began staring at the wallpaper in the nook. It was a sort of red plaid on cream, very dirty and stained and oppressive. Pale green, I thought, was a nice color . . . I rushed into Virginia's (ex) room, grabbed a brush and a can of paint, and managed to cover every inch of the hideous paper before dinnertime. Now I am sitting here looking into the kitchen, where there is some wallpaper I have loathed ever since we moved in. It is covered with a fruit design in dark, muddy primary colors—red for cherries, strawberries, and apples; blue for grapes and plums; and a mustard yellow for peaches, pears, and pineapples. All this fruitery is tastefully interspersed with large gray compotes and parfait bowls, and the only thing that has preserved it so far is the fact that ours is a very large kitchen and I am a woman of small courage. A nice pale-green wall would look lovely in there . . . and now that I notice it, the kitchen chairs need painting . . . and there's the downstairs toilet, which is that horrid pink . . . and the upstairs bath, which is an indeterminate color, a yellowish-gray or grayish-yellow, rather like a jaundiced elephant. I see now that I must watch myself carefully or the entire house will be the same pale green. Well, as Wayne said, watching me in the nook, "At least it's not *orange*."

Jill is watching the men pour cement down a chute into the basement. The truck missed my pet azalea but flattened a couple of snapdragons (I think they're snapdragons—I can't tell yet; they aren't in bloom) Wayne just set out the other day. I have been painting furiously, hoping that my progress will compensate for the loss. The workmen had enough trouble getting the truck close enough to work the chute through the old coalbin window without my rushing out to defend two snapdragons.

The ironing and mending, Virginia's old contributions around here, are piling up like twin Everests; and I am still astonished every evening to discover that I am the one who has to make sandwiches for the school lunches. But I miss, too, her constant and inventive remodeling of her own clothes, her eternal hair washing (surely the most frequently washed hair outside a production of *South Pacific*), and sister Patsy's phone calls, always timed to interrupt dinner.

Something I will never forget: a pair of nylon stockings she gave me for my birthday, one month after she came to live with us. It was an interesting story I overheard her telling her social worker, all about a puppy that had jumped at her from the bushes and clawed her legs and could she please have a voucher for another pair of nylons?

I never said a word.

JUNE

JUNE is the month of romance. In June young brides in a froth of lace gaze from the pages of the magazines, their eyes soft with dreams, and their dreams filled with silver plate, automatic washers and driers, and wall-to-wall broadloom. Oh, romantic love-lured brides, let me tell you the truth about June! June, the month of report cards, of outgrown swim suits, and of elementary school graduation exercises with speeches by the principal, the vice-principal, all teachers who are retiring or moving to other schools, a half-dozen sixth-graders with glazed eyes, frogs in their throats, and sweaty 3 x 5 cards clutched inches from the tips of their noses—and a guest speaker who thinks he is Mort Sahl or Shelley Berman.

June is, moreover, a long, miserable, ineffectual battle with Daylight Saving Time. I have never believed that the proponents of Daylight Saving Time spend their "saved" time lolling on the sand at the beach. No, I rather imagine that at 9 P.M. these people could be found prowling the suburban streets and enjoying the hysterical cries of mothers trying to put schoolchildren to bed in bedrooms where the hot sun blasts through the darkest window shades and the temperature stands at 90° F. And in the morning? Why, in the morning the proponents of Daylight Saving Time bolt their breakfasts so that they can stand at their front windows and watch the children, baggy-eyed and exhausted, stumbling sleepless to school. I hope they're satisfied.

Under the influence of D.S.T., time takes on a shifty and evasive character, and the children—who hate D.S.T. almost as much as their mothers do—regard it as the final unarguable evidence of the untrustworthy, scheming nature of the adult world. There's dishonesty for you; there's deceit. And it doesn't even have the virtue of being a pleasant fable, for example, the Santa Claus myth. Does D.S.T. wear a cute red suit and have a nose like a cherry and bring presents? Does D.S.T. have eight prancing reindeer with only seven names you can remember so that you can make a parlor game out of them, like trying to remember more than six of the Seven Dwarfs? Can you put D.S.T. on a greeting card? Has anybody written a poem about D.S.T., or a song? If they have, I bet it's a dirge.

At eight o'clock bedtime it is really only seven, and the children know it—mark my words, *they know it.*

This is sneaky of me, actually, starting my chapter on June when I never did finish off May properly. Because I didn't—I just stopped. I never got around to telling about Sports Day and watching the fifth-graders do Maypole dances without once getting tangled up, nor about Cameron's weekend camping trip and the new pet he brought home to add to our menagerie—a wild painted turtle named Pender. And I forgot (perhaps intentionally) to chronicle a brief, intoxicating fling at a clever dieting scheme. I allowed myself only as many calories per day as the number of words I wrote on the previous day; but I abandoned the whole thing after I spent one day in an excruciating struggle with a 300-word outline for a half-hour television play. I am still ten pounds overweight.

However, 'tis, 'tis June. Duncan has been reading *Candide* and fighting with Malcolm because he bought popsicles instead of ice-cream bars from the ice-cream man; I have been ironing to harpsichord music by Haydn, which is as close to painless as I can make it; and we are *not* moving anywhere, so I can stop mooning around in a sentimental fashion over every touching crack in the plaster and over the mousehole Malcolm hammered shut with a piece of galvanized tin upstairs. The new basement floor is dry, the new study is painted, and I ran out of paint before I could get around to covering up those pears and plums and pineapples on the kitchen walls.

Me: Did you bite Sandy, Jill?
Jill: No! (howls) She put her thumb in my mouth (howls) *and I wanted my mouth shut!*

The garden was full of grosbeaks the other morning. (Evening grosbeaks, at 8 A.M.—maybe D.S.T. has them confused too?) The males are gorgeous with their black, tangerine, and white plumage and their pistachio-green beaks; they look almost tropical. The bird book says they are yellow, but it isn't a very *yellow* yellow.

The beets are high, the corn is growing, the peas are climbing the chicken-wire netting in our back-yard farm —and I can't get the weeding done because I have hay fever. I never *used* to have hay fever. It's something that's been creeping up on me, a little more each year, like gray hair and crow's-feet. So I've begun sneezing—a little more each year—and I can't go out into the garden unless I take along a pocketful of Kleenex. It isn't *hay* of course, and we don't have ragweed around these parts, so I don't know what causes it. It isn't the syringa any more than it's the peas, and it doesn't matter what part of the garden I go to, the Kleenex has to accompany me. Imagine me at my gardening: I pull a weed, blow my nose, pull a weed, blow my nose, pull a weed, sneeze five times in a row *and* blow my nose. . . .

Virginia has been here to pick up a few of her things and to store her wedding gown with us. My analysis of what she took with her (hardly anything) and what she left (a closet full of dresses) and how she behaved (shy and a little giggly) leads me to an inescapable conclusion —we will be foster grandparents before the snow flies. She wanted to tell me, I think, and she came as close as she could. "I won't be needing these," she said, and I think she knew I knew, and that was enough.

It's Sunday and we are moving furniture again. Every other Sunday, it seems, we are seized by a hysterical fit of furniture moving. We don't attend church, and this may be some kind of spiritual tension building up in us that might otherwise be dissipated with a little hymn singing or fidgeting in uncomfortable pews. However, if you have ever taken care of a hamster or any other small animal, you know how it keeps moving its nest about in whatever quarters you provide for it. Our Juliet, the most engaging golden hamster I have ever met, makes nests of newspaper strips and chewed-up egg cartons, and spends all her spare time—when she is not racking up mileage in the little wheel she got for Christmas—moving these nests around. She has a two-story house made of wood and wire-mesh, and she moves upstairs and down and from corner to corner as fancy takes her.

I don't know whether Juliet is searching for some ultimate perfection in living arrangements, but we are—we adults, that is. The children, on the other hand, seem to be searching only for variety. And a certain amount of variety is necessary. We live in the closets in this house—I mean that literally: *we live in the closets.* For, despite its apparent size, our house has only three bedrooms. That would have worked out (with Virginia) at three occupants per bedroom, but we converted the former dining room into a master bedroom, closing the sliding doors that lead into the front hall and latching them together (we discovered this was necessary when neighbor children began wandering through our bedroom, sometimes when we were still in bed); and we put Virginia in the former sun room at the far end of the living room. That still left six children to be sorted out into three bedrooms upstairs. That sounds handy enough, two per bedroom—that is, it sounds handy to anyone who doesn't know children. It is, however, impossible to sort out six children into three bedrooms and achieve any arrangement that can be called permanent. And it has nothing to do with beds and chests of drawers. Alliances and ententes, animosities and outright hostilities shift from month to month, and the children must be separated and reassembled accordingly.

We have relieved this situation to some extent by occupying the closets. There are five closets upstairs; one is a mere wardrobe but the other four have windows and two of them are large enough to hold a bed, a desk, and a chair. So now we live in two of the closets, put clothing and other things in two, and use the fifth as a study, workshop, or what we call, in family parlance, a "hidey-hole." It's true, once you get a bed, a desk, and a chair into one of these oversized closets you can't exactly cha-cha-cha in the middle of the floor, and in order to clean I stand in the doorway and merely reach in with a dustmop as far as I can. But there is something secret and delightful about a little room with a little window—it always makes me think of Heidi and grow envious—and I wonder if the ideal house for a large family mightn't be one with a series of tiny bedrooms ranged along a corridor rather like a cell block. Architects, consider this.

Togetherness is not anything that we have to strive to foster in this family; it's a little *apartness* that requires the struggle. We have, in fact, explored the ultimate in togetherness: 4,446 miles from here to Ensenada and back with eight of us in a station wagon and all sleeping together in a 9 x 15-foot tent. When we laid out air mattresses and sleeping bags in that tent at night, it left one narrow corridor down the middle to the door, just large enough for the centerpole, the electric lantern, and all the things we tried to read while jockeying for the little bit of light the lantern gave—comic books, magazines, travel folders, maps, and the daily paper. Those who were most likely to leave the tent at night were positioned nearest the door. I think the most helpful comment I can give concerning this mode of travel to any family considering something similarly foolhardy is this: it can be done.

We have never found a child who can withstand for any long period of time the psychological and physical onslaught of rooming with Duncan. The basic law of child dynamics in our household is, *Duncan tends to expand.* We have tried having him room with another boy, dividing the room in two with an imaginary line, a bed on each side, desk and drawers on each side. But an imaginary line is insufficient; Duncan's bed creeps inexorably across the floor, his belongings follow it, and he begins to stack radio parts on the other boy's desk and old copies of *Popular Electronics* under the other boy's bed. Once we tried stringing a wire across the center of the room and hanging heavy draperies from it; but after the first few days of this plan, anyone sighting down the center line could plainly see that the draperies hung down only so far and then bent suddenly sideways under the thrust of Duncan's perambulating bed.

This is not like national aggression; he is not trying deliberately to pre-empt all available space at the expense of others. But he fills any room to the corners with his effects, his noise, his ideas, and his ego. The basement is impossible. I have fought a constant battle to keep Duncan contained in something a bit less than three-quarters of the basement area, but he keeps seeping out. He has a huge old kitchen cabinet full of chemistry and photographic equipment, a table with the photographic enlarger on it, a smaller table for auxiliary trays and bottles; and all last winter whenever I went down to get something out of the freezer I found that he had commandeered the top of that, too, and tools and bottles had to be moved before I could get at raspberries for dinner. I know how the natives feel when the jungle keeps marching into the clearing and has to be chopped back with machetes.

The new basement floor having dried by now, Duncan is engaged in moving all his radio equipment from his upstairs radio shack (one of the windowed closets) down to the nether regions. The major reason for this is that Duncan is getting older and staying up later and his friends are getting bigger and their voices louder and their feet heavier on the stairs, and Polly and Jill have consequently been losing sleep. So the cigar boxes and biscuit tins and jars full of transistors, resistors, condensers, tubes, and miscellaneous unidentifiable (by me) pieces of radios are being transported downward, along with speakers, batteries, old radio cabinets, and several miles of snarled wires. I have carefully pointed out the area within which all this must be penned, so that a little room would be left for Andy's model airplane building and Mac's and Cam's miscellaneous carpentry, but I am not sure he was really listening.

The three smaller boys are engaged in the construction and decoration of a clubhouse. They have cleaned out the shed beneath the sun room and have installed a makeshift floor, and they are painting various legends on the walls (inside and out of sight, thank heavens), things like DIG MAN DIG, GO MAN GO, and KOOKIE KOOKIE LEND ME YOUR COMB. They are calling it a rock-and-roll club, although prospects of doing much more than tapping a foot to music are rather limited; the ceiling is so low that not even Cameron can stand erect inside the room.

As if hay fever weren't enough to bear, I am now suddenly afflicted with a patch of itching misery on the palm of my right hand which has turned out to be eczema. I've never had eczema before in my life, either. I am dosing it with something that smells like acid shortstop that you dip photographic prints in after the developer, and smearing it afterwards with zinc oxide, but I don't see any results. I make a very poor one-handed housewife.

In fact, I make a poor two-handed housewife, most of the time.

Every month I read the women's magazines, hunting

for something that will help me with my housekeeping problems. I search through the magazines I get as I trundle my cart up to the supermarket cash register, I leaf through the big, glossy magazines on the stands at the drugstore; but I haven't found what I need—not yet.

I've found all kinds of other things. I've learned how to remove every conceivable kind of identifiable spot—it's just too bad my children specialize in spots nobody can identify. I've learned how to paint an old piano to look like a piece of awning or how to cover it with wallpaper to make the room look larger—we don't have a piano, though. I've learned how to arrange dried grasses, dead branches, and old hunks of driftwood into stunning Japanese-style flower arrangements—but what do you do with twenty-eight dandelions with stems one and a half inches long? I've learned how to make a handy pencil container for my desk out of an old frozen orange juice can touched up with paint. It isn't the magazine's fault I never have any pencils—how can anybody with six children have pencils?

What I want to find out, really, is something nobody seems to touch on. The question is one that a friend asked me once, and I had no answer to give her, and it has been bothering me ever since. What I want to know is, how do you dust a bird's nest?

You can blow on it, I know that. And it works, up to a point, with robins' nests and sparrows' nests. But it can be fatal with hummingbirds' nests—they never look the same, once you've had to use scotch tape. Besides, it seems like a treacherous method to start using; it can lead to blowing on books, blowing on shelves, blowing on bric-a-brac, banisters, newel posts, the top of the television set. Whoo, I'm out of breath already and the dust's flying all over the house!

Actually, although I have two old nests on my window-sill at the moment, the question is more symbolic than literal. What I really mean is, how do you live graciously when you have a stuffed deer head with its antlers painted pink mounted on the porch beside the front door? How do you achieve that serene uncluttered look when two boys are making kites on the living-room rug and your six-year-old daughter has changed her shoes four times and left each pair in a different room and your three-year-old daughter is rolling out plasticene snakes on the coffee table? How do you prepare an elegant dinner when several small boys are standing around in the kitchen making impressions of their hands in pie tins full of wet plaster of Paris?

I like the idea of gracious living. I can imagine myself in a swishy skirt and a low-necked embroidered sweater, handing a tray of elaborate tidbits to my guest. There is a bowl of flowers on the coffee table, the carpet is impeccably vacuumed, the draperies hang in precise folds, candles burn on the mantelpiece. I love to imagine myself that way. I hate to imagine myself in jeans and an old shirt, with a dirty cloth in one hand and a can of wax in the other, and the draperies down and the rug rolled up, and my shoes off and I've just been out in the kitchen where I gutted a salmon and put it in the oven, so I smell fishy as well as waxy—and there's my husband in the front hall and my guest (the one I didn't know I was going to have) standing right behind him, staring at me. Well, I hate to imagine that, but I don't have to *imagine* it anyway; I only have to *remember* it. It happened.

When I can't find any answers in the household hints I look at the pictures. I like the pictures, the full-color advertisements with the blush-pink kitchens and the pale-blue living rooms with the stunning fuchsia cushions strewn so tastefully here and there. But that woman, in her drip-dry dress or her skintight matador pants, doesn't she have a child who makes plasticene snakes on the coffee table? Where, in that room, is the old Batman comic strewn tastefully on the rug? Where is the bouquet of dandelions with inch-and-a-half stems? Where does such a woman put the stuffed deer head with the pink antlers that her eleven-year-old son retrieved from the neighbor's trash? Where are the discarded shoes, the pieces of kite string, the smear of peanut butter across Perry Como's face on the TV screen? What has she done with the lumpy ashtrays made in fifth-grade art class and the sweater that belongs to the boy across the street, which he left hanging over the lampshade? Where is the beef bone the dog sneaked into the house and left under the settee in the corner? Where are the carrot tops sprouting in saucers of water and the stubborn avocado seed that refuses to sprout at all? Where are the feathers from the last bird the cat brought in, and who had time to pick up all those broken color crayons?

Don't tell me how to remove berry stains by pouring boiling water through the cloth. Don't tell me how to make cute little checkerboard sandwiches for forty people or how to use a set of shoe pockets in ten fascinating ways. But, about that woman . . . Even if she *has* taken her children to the basement and left them bound and gagged for the last three hours or so, I still want to know, where does she keep *her* birds' nests, and how does she dust them?

The children are in bed, and I ought to be there too, but we seem to have promised them an overnight camping trip this weekend and the job of packing things is always mine. I must, I suppose, sit down and start by making a list. . . .

If I can get my mind on it, that is. We went to Andy's graduation banquet—as spectators, not eaters; they feed the children first and then the parents arrive for the ceremonies. I was somewhat consoled by the knowledge that next year Cameron will only be in the fifth grade, and after three graduations in a row we'll get to skip one. The speeches were no better than usual, but they were at least broken up by a nice demonstration of square-dancing from the sixth-graders in the square-dance club. The general tenor of the remarks is always the same: A students are fine and B students are perhaps even better, having provided the competition to force those A students to work hard, but it's the C students who are the Real Backbone of the School, the salt of the earth, the hope of the nation, et cetera. The first time I heard all this I thought perhaps I misunderstood it, but the second time my impression was confirmed. It is always interesting to watch the poor handful of A students standing on the platform and reaping their rewards for all that hard work—abuse (you are not perfect and don't get cocky), left-handed praise (you wouldn't be here if it weren't for those B students pushing you up from below), and a hearty depreciation of their accomplishments (scholarship isn't everything, remember that). I realize this saves the egos of all those C students from irreparable damage and wards off the formation of an intellectual elite, but it's no wonder Sputnik got there first.

Andy, who is not an A student, had his moment of glory when his name was called as one of the two sixth-grade students voted best in citizenship by the faculty. He didn't quite believe his ears and had to be urged on stage by his table companions; and it was no wonder he was surprised, for it was just that morning he went to the music room to recite ten verses of Psalm 2 as punishment for horsing around in music class, and he was feeling pretty wicked and depraved as a consequence. I have never quite understood the reasoning behind this use of the Bible as a punishing medium. It seems a fine stroke of antireligion to me, especially since the content of the memorized verses has little to do with either the misdemeanor or the child. A few lines of the telephone directory might be more effective; but I suppose we couldn't risk having anybody regard the *telephone directory* with distaste!

We had just finished eating ice cream at home and watching Andy open two science-fiction books by way of a modest graduation present when the phone rang. It was Virginia's social worker. He talked for a while about Virginia, but I had a feeling there was some other motive behind the call, and finally he wormed his way around to it. Would we want to take another child, a twelve-year-old part-Chinese girl?

A *lovely little twelve-year-old part-Chinese girl*, that's what he said.

I said *no*.

Don't think I didn't have a weak moment. For a few seconds I cast about wildly, mentally stowing her in this room and that room, doubling the boys up here and there . . .

No, I said.

I reported the conversation to Wayne, who for some inexplicable reason reported it to the children, and they all came storming into my room in protest. They could double up, Andy could move in with Duncan, there was plenty of room . . . They hopped up and down, insisting it would be "so interesting" to have another child, and (as Duncan put it) "we could stand a little excitement around here," so why not?

But if they are not willing to face my limitations as a mother, I am. I put them off and sent them to bed.

I am still sneezing and doctoring my poor eczematous paw.

Home again, exhausted, and mostly from sneezing; but the children had a wonderful time on our overnight camping trip, floating around on the river with air mattresses. Nobody but me noticed that the people camping behind us must have tied their puppy to one of our tent stakes, and that three large boys arrived on bicycles at midnight and each one was convinced that his two companions were deaf, and that the road leading to the highway was being used for a 2 A.M. drag race.

I used to marvel how motherhood instantly sharpens the nighttime ear. I could spring up wide awake from a sound sleep at the slightest noise from the baby's crib. Only now I don't really have to any more, it would be handier to be like my husband who has a deaf ear and can sleep on the good one. (What puppy? What drag race?)

Every time there was a lull in the conversation, somebody (usually Duncan) introduced the question, "Why can't we have another foster child?" They, of course, can't see that having children around is any work at all. But my chance came when Duncan asked the same question while we were in the car, parked in a little town where Wayne had gotten out to look at the advertisements in the local real-estate offices. We were in the car along with the tent, the eight sleeping bags, the ice chest, the air mattresses, the beach ball with air still in it, a carton of pots and pans, a canvas bag full of wet swim suits, and the children all quarreling furiously over whose turn it was to sit where. "Why can't we have another foster child?" Duncan asked.

"If we had one," I said, "*then where would she sit?*"

Wayne has got island fever again. He would like to buy an island, or a piece of an island, or failing that, just a bit of beach somewhere, or even a small stretch of riverbank. The last lot we had, a nice stretch of wooded beach on a sheltered bay, we sold to get enough money for the down payment on our house. (I wrote a story about this but the editors thought it was depressing, selling a lot in order to buy a house; it never occurred to them we were darned lucky to have anything at all to sell.) Anyway, for four years we haven't had any summer place; the only other property we own is a couple of lots in Seaside, California. But don't let that name fool you, because our property is a long way from the side of the sea and there's nothing on the place at all, not even a tree for shade. In fact, if there's any shade it comes from the big fence around Fort Ord, a few yards away. But the deed, yellow with age, is fully of lovely old Spanish names and signed by a Land Commissioner named Steinbeck, and the taxes run around $3 a year, so we like owning it.

Did you know that men with Blood Type O are the most dangerous kind? Very fertile, I mean. And marriages in which both partners are the same type—AA, OO, BB, et cetera—are more fertile than others? Wayne was reading all this in some journal or other and showed it to me. He's O, of course, but we didn't know about me, so I phoned the doctor and asked him to look it up on my chart, which he did.

I'm O, too.

Tomorrow is the last day of school. The house is rapidly filling up with scribblers, Work Books for Young Explorers, and great sheets of paper with crayoned pictures from art class. What are parents supposed to do with all this? You can't save it all, nor can you callously throw it out as soon as it arrives. Wayne has a large file of pieces of art work, and I have a thick manila envelope stuffed with report cards. Upstairs in the linen cupboard there are stacks of scribblers, including the notebook in which Duncan did 1,500 arithmetic problems from a third-grade arithmetic book the year he was in Grade One. But there must be a limit to all this saving. It will have to stop sooner or later.

Sooner, I think, when I look at that linen cupboard. If I ever have any money to buy more linens (even if I did I'd find something more interesting to spend it on), I wouldn't know where to put them anyway. I have a lovely big linen cupboard with double doors that open to reveal several shelves a foot and a half deep and over five feet long. You could store a dozen blankets there, and sheets galore, and heaps of fluffy bath towels in rainbow colors, just like in the ads. *You* could, that is. What I've got in there is another matter: old scribblers, curtain rods, that hideous oil painting of the now-distinguished Negro writer, boxes of Christmas-tree ornaments, two cartons of outgrown baby clothes and scraps of cloth meant to be made into doll clothing. The two middle shelves are reserved for the linens—about eight extra sheets, a few limp pillowcases, and two piles of bath towels—all of them shoved down to one end to make room for the surplus rocks and shells out of Malcolm's rock and shell collections. The only reason we keep on calling it the linen cupboard is that I can't think of anything else to call it that would bear repeating.

It is raining and everybody has passed into the next grade. Wayne's one good suit is at the tailor's, where the poor man is valiantly trying to reweave the shabby edges. Cam's shoes need heels, any day now the driver will deliver our rug and the bill for cleaning it. (I'm going to roll it up and put it in the basement for the summer, because all it does is fill up with sand from now until September, anyway.) And every time Wayne comes in the door he's bought something at the hardware store to repair things around here. I've just been checking the budget, and *something* has got to give.

Furthermore, I just found out that *we have eaten our new fence.*

However, Malcolm has been made a squad leader in the Junior Forest Wardens and has passed his first-aid exam at St. John's Ambulance, and a colleague of Wayne's has dumped the leftover contents of his larder here on the eve of his departure for New York. He seems to have lived on pickles and chutney, but the *pièce de resistance* is a bottle of gin and some tonic. Do you suppose gin is good for eczema and hay fever?

JULY

JULY has begun and the year is half over. Never mind all that "good old summertime" stuff, July is not a month I am overly fond of. For one thing, it is a time of relaxation, disorganization, and lack of schedule—and to keep all these relaxed, disorganized, unscheduled people fed, clothed, and cleaned-up-after has me running. At least in the winter they are out of the house for specified, reliable times of the day. But in July somebody is always hungry, clothes are always dirty, swim suits are always wadded up in wet balls for me to untwist and rinse out, and the children use a dozen bath towels a day not counting the ones they lose at the community pool or leave in neighbors' back yards. July is tent-sleeping time, a time of mislaid socks and grass-stained pajamas; and at 11:45 at night I am out in the back yard hissing fiercely, "You kids shut up and stop making so much noise or you're coming right into the house!"

Nobody comes to meals on time in July, and the kitchen linoleum is sprinkled with sugar and dotted with dirty drips of Kool-aid. "Dump the sand out of your shoes before you come in!" I cry, but there are little hills of sand by the children's beds upstairs, and more in the bathroom, and still more in the boys' trouser pockets, along with mashed crab shells, pea pods left over from eating raw peas in the garden, and a few gummy, scrunched-up popsicle wrappers. The girls wake up too early when the sun strikes their east-facing windows, and the boys go to sleep too late on the other side of the house. Doors are always open, which means that children who formerly knocked now simply walk in. Our downstairs bathroom becomes a Public Convenience Station, and I discover that other people's children don't know any more about lifting seats or flushing toilets than mine do.

The transparent apples become ripe in July, and every morning the children gather enough to fill one of those supermarket bags—you know, the kind that used to hold $5 worth of groceries but now hold $10 worth, which shows you that at least the American packaging industry hasn't been standing still even though the bags give every appearance of being the same size as they used to be. We eat as many of these apples as we can without becoming ill, and the rest are stewed up into applesauce or sliced into apple pie. Nobody asks "What's for dessert?" until that tree is finished.

On the first of July Canadians celebrate, but not very much, their national holiday. This is the Canadian Fourth of July but it resembles the American Fourth the way tap water resembles vodka. I have been trying for eight years to analyze the Canadian attitude toward holidays, and as far as I can tell the main thing about a Canadian holiday is that you get a day off from work. Canadians are very careful and scrupulous about that; when they say holiday they mean holiday, and you don't get a daily paper or *anything*. On the other hand, you rarely see any festive signs of the holiday itself. I think everybody just goes to sleep on the davenport with a newspaper over his face. Yesterday's newspaper, of course.

Living in a foreign country—even if we are just 45 minutes north of the border—brings out the dormant patriot in me. Still, there are some wonderful things about Canada: the wilderness that begins practically at the city limits here and stretches—with a few dots of human habitation—all the way to the North Pole; "Alouette" and "Le Raftsman"; and the feeling of history I get whenever I shop at Hudson's Bay Company and read the legend under the name, "Incorporated 2nd May 1670," which makes me feel I should slap my pile of beaver pelts on the counter and ask for sugar, flour, tea, and gunpowder, instead of merely tendering my charge plate for a pair of nylons.

Living in even so faintly a foreign country gives us good practice in raising nonconformists. The when-in-Rome principle is not the one I live by, though I suppose it has its virtues. We are, for one thing, quite frankly a family of atheists, and it is not fashionable to be atheistic or even agnostic in these times. It is perhaps even less fashionable in Canada than it is in the United States, for here the Bible is read every morning in the public schools—though, as a sop to Catholicism, it is neither interpreted nor explained; it is simply read. The children dutifully recite the Lord's Prayer: "Our Father which art in Heaven,

Halloween be Thy name," as one of them told us some years ago. I was astonished at this when Duncan first started school here, and in my ignorance of Canadian mores I went to speak to the teacher. I asked her if they really read the Bible to these children every morning. "Why, yes," she told me, and then added with blithe assurance, "but it's strictly nondenominational."

"But we aren't Christians," I said.

She had, apparently, never thought of this. She asked if I wanted to have Duncan excused from the room during the reading. I said no, I didn't think it mattered much under the circumstances. I was borne out in this; I've discovered that the children let this morning Bible reading pass by them unremarked, just a part of the routine, like sharpening pencils or erasing the blackboard. They have learned not to listen. But I suppose the irony of this is lost upon the advocates of morning Bible reading.

I was, simply, raised an atheist. I cut my teeth on Ingersoll's lectures. I had never seen the inside of a church until I was fifteen, when I accompanied a friend to a Sunday-school picnic (at which I won a small Bible for high hurdles or maybe it was the broad jump, I don't remember—but I still have the Bible). It would have been ironic if this had changed my life, in a kind of reversal of what happened to my mother at the same age. She had been a stanch Catholic, until one morning she arrived at the church for Mass and wondered "What am I doing this for, anyway?" She walked around the block three times pondering the question and then went home, never to go again. However, I didn't go near a church again until I was in college, and then a bunch of us spent a few weeks' worth of Sundays attending various churches out of what I suppose was mere curiosity. Then again I forgot about religion, and except for two or three weddings my only contacts with the spiritual life have been brief arguments with the Jehovah's Witnesses who arrive at the door on Saturdays and Sundays and press tracts upon me with the tireless insistence of a hostess passing cookies at a tea.

I have never felt that religion is necessary to ethics and morals. I can fill out my income-tax form honestly without leaning on God, and I can also look into the starry sky and contemplate the vast complexity and marvelous order of the universe without concluding that it must have had a Creator. They said, of course, that there were no atheists in foxholes—that was during World War II—and from the astonishing rate at which eminent literary figures are converted during their declining years, one might assume that there are not any atheists on deathbeds either. From a statistical point of view the death rate of atheists must be significantly lower than that of the rest of the population, and it occurs to me that the longer I cling to atheism the longer I shall perhaps survive. In fact, I might get overlooked altogether, who knows?

If ministers' children are sometimes atheists, I wonder what atheists' children turn out to be? I have a sister (perhaps she never read Ingersoll) who is up to her eyebrows in church activity.

But I have often puzzled over why some people speak incessantly of the church but never mention religion or God.

The boys are outside having the time of their lives in the digging patch by the swings. They have landscaped it into a town, with roads, an airport, a ranch, a lake, a river (fed by the hose), and there are about eight of them out there with toy airplanes, miniature cars, animals, farm buildings, fences, a garage with gas pumps, and various other items, some so small that I am certain they will be buried by the end of the day and will never be seen again. Except where a mountain has been covered with a snowfall of all-purpose white flour sifted from my flour sifter, the dirt is very black and very dirty, but they love it. As for me, my pleasure at seeing them so happily engaged is doubled by the security of knowing that down in the basement I have that automatic washer and drier. Those things have made a nicer mother of me.

I still have hay fever and I still have eczema and the only thing that makes it bearable is that I think occasionally of poor Dostoevsky. *He* had hemorrhoids and epilepsy.

It's Sunday afternoon. Wayne has finally found one of the polliwogs that had escaped and was wandering dustily about on the floor in direst peril of death by squashing, and I have ironed enough clothes to last out the coming week. On Friday morning we are going to leave for a camping trip, all around the Olympic Peninsula, and I am deep in a list of things to take (including antihistamine tablets, Kleenex, zinc oxide, nasal spray—good grief, I'm going to be traveling like Glenn Gould with a suitcase full of nostrums and remedies) and things to do before we go (like leave a note for the milkman, give the key to Jerry so he can feed the dog and cat and water the plants and bring in the mail that's too big for the mail slot, find all the bicycles and put them in the basement, turn down the thermostat on the water heater). Why is it that every time we go anywhere nobody else has to give it a thought until the morning of the day we're supposed to leave? But me, I'm running around doing things for a week beforehand.

One thing I've got to do is to mend about a dozen pairs of jeans. I'm *not* going to do laundry en route.

Wayne is going to Mexico City between Christmas and New Year's, to attend some annual professional meetings, and not only that, but there are more meetings in Vienna a year from now. The university usually chips in financially on such matters but I can still see the $$ in red ink floating phantasmagorically before my eyes. Never mind, I also have the perfect solution: I am going to start a movement to have the meetings of all professional societies held in the dead of winter and in the middle of South Dakota. This will provide a true and reliable test of interests and loyalties—and will incidentally help balance a few budgets here and there across the continent, not to mention mine.

I don't know what to do, however, about island fever. He simply won't be content until we own a stretch of beach with salt water lapping it. A whole island, complete, is what he really wants, but in lieu of that a fraction of an island will have to do. There are several waterfront lots on one of the San Juan islands which his father told us about not long ago—perhaps the last reasonably priced waterfront we'll ever hear about. I think I'll have to ask whether it's still available.

Malcolm has won his first-aid badge at St. John's Ambulance; he didn't miss a single Saturday morning class and he passed the exam. Now why can't he apply some of that spirit to *schoolwork?*

Hah! I sat down yesterday afternoon and wrote—all at one sitting—a humorous short-short story called "An

Impersonal Third Party," all about a pleasingly plump wife whose husband can't convince her that he likes her that way. Wher*ever* do I get my ideas?

Our peas are ripe, the corn is 18 inches high, and the beans are climbing the bean poles. But the weeds—! Oh, and by the way, I've started to sneeze *in* the house, too (you ought to see me trying to cut the boys' hair while in the throes of a sneezing attack).

But it is, in my case, only a comic ailment. I don't need sympathy; all I need is Kleenex.

Some citizens are waiting to hear from the little green men in flying saucers. I'm not. I get enough communications from little people, although my little people aren't green and they weren't brought by a flying saucer, not by a long shot. And I suppose that from an intergalactic or even an interplanetary point of view their communications are not of vast and vital importance.

But I find the stuff, in an intramural way, fairly absorbing.

There are, in the first place, the standard, regularized, direct communications. Christmas lists, for example, are tendered in grubby pencil, much erased. Such lists range from the touching simplicity of "a new doll" to the outrageous insolence of a list complete with catalogue numbers and list prices. Duncan usually gets his list back again with a parental request for a downward revision. Why he asks for such expensive presents (usually some trifling bit of radio-electronics equipment) is something we dull parents have never been able to grasp, especially because we find it so easy to submit such modest little lists of our own for the children's use: a new pencil, some paper clips, a typewriter ribbon. We were just lucky to have been born with simple tastes, I guess.

In addition to lists, other direct communications include the notes passed downstairs from sickabeds: "Mom can I have paste and sizzors?" or "I don't like that soup do I got to eat it?" or, boldly and toward the end of the illness, "Mom can I come down and watch TV?"

But these are the communications directed at me, and they are limited by the demands of the situation and the parent-child relationship. What I find more revealing in my daily study of the little people is the rest of their written material: memos, signs, threats and warnings, bedside jottings, and little scraps of paper wadded deep in the bottoms of trouser pockets, bearing significant legends such as "Duncan is a dirty bum." Now, the legend "Duncan is a dirty bum" may never have reached the eyes of its subject. But I don't doubt that the mere writing of it must have satisfied some deeply felt need; it may even have averted a fight, although if Duncan had run across it, he might well have started one himself.

Signs such as "FOX CLUB, Members Only, All Others Keep Out" appear frequently. And there are many codes and ciphers, usually much too elaborate to be of practical use. I find, most frequently, a sweat-stained piece of paper with the code laboriously set out on it, and perhaps one sentence done in the code which when deciphered generally reads something like "Duncan is a dirty bum." No further messages in that code will be discovered.

More cryptic than the codes and less decipherable than the ciphers are some of the memos I discover under pillows when changing the bedding, or behind chests of drawers when attempting a thorough cleaning. "Vois beebs 34" on a torn corner of tablet paper would have baffled me indefinitely had I not faced its author and admitted my defeat (another chink in my parental armor of I-understand-what-you-are-up-to-perfectly). Cameron explained, tolerantly, that a certain radio station was having a contest and one could win it by phoning in with the exact number of times a certain record went BEEP. "Vois," he said after some thought, was *voice*; but he had forgotten why the word was there at all.

I find IOU's, too, and sometimes I uncover long-standing debts of which I have had no previous knowledge, despite the fact that all financial deals are supposed to be cleared with HQ. But the power of putting it on paper is such that when a recent wager of the more extravagant sort ("I'll betcha a *million dollars!*") proved disastrous for the bettor, and when the taker demanded payment, the issue was apparently settled amicably enough by a piece of paper which I later found. It was a receipt, carefully inscribed, for one million dollars—a moral victory if not a financial one.

The written word, indeed, carries a great deal of weight around here. There are two typewriters in the house, under pretty constant attack by the two adult members of the family. Sometimes things get so thick, in fact, that the other day our almost-seven-year-old Polly decided that the only real way to engage my attention was on paper. I received her note: "Dear Mommy, I love you, How are your storys? Love Polly."

Not all the communications are on paper, of course. We are still trying to find out who scratched a Z (for Zorro, naturally) on the top of one of Duncan's old radio cabinets; and Virginia was a confirmed wall-beside-the-telephone doodler.

Remember the clubhouse the boys made out of the

shed underneath the sun porch, only last month, and how they climaxed the entire operation by painting KOOKIE KOOKIE LEND ME YOUR COMB and DIG MAN DIG all over the walls? When the paint was dry they asked me to come and look, and I allowed as how it looked pretty good, but I wondered what it was going to look like after they'd used it for a while. I needn't have wondered; last time I looked in, just yesterday, somebody had parked a bicycle inside, but otherwise it was as bare and clean as it was when they finally put the lid on the paint can and inadvertently slopped the wet brushes across their trousers. I don't think they've been inside there for three weeks. Well, I've been thinking about this and I've developed a new theory of anthropological importance. People have been brooding for a long time about the cave paintings—why they are in those narrow, hard-to-squirm-into back alleys of the caves, and what they were for. Now I know. Religious rituals? Nothing of the sort; there were a bunch of cave kids, bored to death on a rainy day, and they asked their mom and dad if they could have a clubhouse, you know, way in the back there, where the cave was too small to be of any use anyway. Why, sure they could. So they crawled back in there and got to work, but they didn't have anything like DIG MAN DIG to put on the walls. They had HUNT MAN HUNT, only in pictures. And that's what they are: the wall decorations for the Hairy Mammoth Club.

I bet they never went back in once it was done, either.

We've done it. We're buying a lot on Henry Island for $200 down and $25 a month. Exactly where this $200 is coming from I'm not too sure, but I've been juggling figures around and cutting budgetary corners here and there and I think we can squeeze by with just a little of that skin of our teeth scraped off. The children, excitedly scanning the map, are expecting us to pack up and go there immediately; but we had to confess that you can't even get there without a boat. Henry Island is mainly uninhabited—what a lovely thought, these days!—and lies off the northwestern end of San Juan Island, a few miles from the International Boundary as it zigzags around the tip of Vancouver Island. Without a boat we'll just have to stand on the beach at San Juan and look longingly across, that's all. Still, it's an investment, and if the current boom in small boating continues we can't go wrong with a piece of beach. Either somebody who buys a boat will buy our piece of beach from us and we'll make a profit, or else we'll succumb to the boom in small boating ourselves—and take a loss. Men with island fever always have boat fever too.

I sat yesterday and put umpteen knees and seats in pairs of blue jeans. A well-patched crew leaves Friday morning for our camping trip. There is something just a little teentsy bit screw-loose about a family with shabby, patched jeans investing in real estate; but we have never pretended to be truly sensible about money, anyway.

Jill's fourth birthday is coming up. Four little girls have been invited, and with Polly and Jill that will make six. Cameron has asked if he can bake the cake and "manage" the party, and if you think *I* opposed the idea you're crazy!

We took six days and five nights for our circuit of the Olympic Peninsula, that wonderful, wildest, westernmost tip of our native land. You can do it in much less, of course, but I can't imagine why. Even our pace wasn't leisurely enough, and at every campsite the children clamored to stay just one more night. We went 833 miles in all, spent $81, ate like loggers, had time each day for a hike of some sort, and chose a week of perfect weather to do it in. My hay fever vanished with my first breath of mountain air up on Hurricane Ridge and it didn't return until we drove back into the driveway at home, which makes me suspect that it's psychosomatic after all—except that I like it here at home, too.

Mountains affect me as catnip affects a cat. Despite my ten pounds of overweight and my advancing years, I am transformed into a mountain goat and want to go leaping about, higher and higher, and never come down again. Which reminds me that in the high school annual of my senior year, my idea of the Ideal Life is listed as "A Swiss chalet, a typewriter, and reams of paper." Here it is twenty years later and I don't think I've changed very much, though I might settle for a forest-fire lookout tower.

I'm not going to rave in detail about the Olympic Peninsula. I can just imagine what it would be like if everybody came rushing out there, dropping tin cans and yellow film cartons and pieces of tinfoil and smoldering cigarette butts all over the place. *Stay home,* unless you are as fanatical as I am about housekeeping in the out-of-doors, for I stand by ready to clobber the kids if they drop so much as a wrapper from an individual piece of Dentyne Chewing Gum, and the only things they are ever allowed to throw out of car windows are prune pits. I guess I figure they might take root and grow, who knows? Cigarette butts are no problem; we don't smoke. (That's how come we're so rich as we are—it's all the money we've saved by not smoking and not going to the barber. It's a small fortune—wherever it is.)

It's afternoon, and Jill's party is in full swing out in the back yard—and here I sit, a lady of leisure, thanks to

Cameron. He is serving the cake he baked, a magnificent thing covered with coconut and shiny dragées, and much too good to be wasted on six little girls who will pick off the dragées, lick at the frosting, and throw away the cake. The presents have been opened: ruffled panties from Kimberley, socks from Sandy, a doll and some bubble bath from Penny, a watering can and some plastic beads like sections of macaroni from Corinne (I can already imagine picking them up off the floor, or, worse, stepping on them at night in my bare feet). The sun is shining mightily and a small breeze keeps blowing the balloons, tied to the wires where the blackberry vine twines along over their heads, back against the thorns; every once in a while the babble of voices is interrupted by a loud BANG! I have been out to supervise the candle-lighting and blowing-out, and to take a few snapshots, but there seems to be nothing else for me to do, except look out the window and notice that they are now playing London Bridge. Cameron is standing by beaming as fatuously as if he were twenty years older than the most of them, rather than a mere five-plus.

I seem to have been baking pies, making applesauce, rinsing out sandy swim suits, and swabbing sun lotion on small backs for hours on end. The days pass with lunches at the beach (and Duncan, who lives in the basement with his radio stuff and has to be dragged forcibly out of doors, gets parboiled and it serves him right), fishing expeditions down at the river (most fish caught are promptly thrown back, and any brought home are eventually buried, for that river at that particular place is not my idea of a sanitary source of food supply), and long afternoons of reading and drinking innumerable glasses of iced tea or lemonade. Andy has been pouring all his allowance into gas-engine model planes that crack up as soon as they leave the ground. Cameron has just finished a huge outline map of the world in India ink and has tacked it up on the wall of his room. "What are you making it for?" Wayne asked him. "Oh—just as a sample of my work," said Cam, carefully lettering CAMERON'S INTERNATIONAL MAP OF THE WORLD inside a fancy legend scroll. This map-drawing hobby doesn't cost Cameron a cent (he uses Wayne's paper, from a big roll in the basement) and he can pour all *his* allowance into his Canadian stamp collection. There is something canny about that boy.

Cherry pie in the oven, cookies baked, laundry whirling in the basement, Duncan fiddling with a hi-fi amplifier in the living room and blaring Brahms at top volume, small girls in the plastic pool, wet footprints leading into the bathroom from the back door—a typical July afternoon. Malcolm and Cameron spent the weekend at the Forest Warden Conservation and Survival Training Camp at Pt. Atkinson, and we drove out to pick them up last night. We watched while they awarded the camp badges for proficiency tests; Malcolm, of course, won every available badge, and again I found myself shaking my head and wondering why he can't do that sort of thing at school. Cameron swore the camp had been "mostly KP" and asserted he "would never go again." But I am immune to such declarations and I notice that he spent the entire morning putting together a survival kit in an old metal 4 x 5 file-card box: matches, fishhooks, powdered soup, tea, coffee, sugar, salt, halazone tablets (left over from World War II in the Pacific), vitamin capsules, a chocolate bar, and raisins—and some of these things he even bought at the store with his allowance. I gather that camp was not as miserable an experience as he tried to make out it was.

Cameron, in fact, had a moment of sheer triumph at

camp when they had Challenge Night and one boy offered a bottle of pop to anyone who could assume a certain yoga position. He hadn't reckoned with Cameron, and those hours of yoga practice last February when the TV set was at the repair shop have finally paid off.

We tried to get a coherent account of what they did and learned at camp, but their major narrative effort so far has gone into a recounting of the horrid ghost stories told in the bunkhouse after Lights Out, especially one called "The Golden Arm." And when I think of it, perhaps that aspect of camping is just as important as lessons in knot tying and tree identification.

I am thinking again of that Swiss chalet, the typewriter, and the reams of paper. Sometimes life rises up around my ears and I have this urge to escape, to go off somewhere perfectly alone where I can get my thoughts in order, where I can peel off these layers of Mother, Dietician, Cook, Laundress, Charwoman, Accountant, Purchasing Agent, Social Convener, and Animal Caretaker, and rediscover that little kernel of Just Me that might still be hiding down in there somewhere. On the other hand, I might discover there's nothing there at all. Maybe I am, after all, nothing but the roles I play.

Two roles I don't get enough time for: (1) Writer; (2) Wife.

I love to sit in a restaurant—even a Greasy Spoon—and have a cup of coffee and a piece of raisin pie à la mode with my husband. That may not seem romantic to you, but after a few weeks around here it is as wickedly tempting as an assignation.

Cameron has just kissed me good night. This doesn't happen very often. All the other boys have outgrown such demonstrations and I suppose if they hadn't we'd be thinking dark Freudian thoughts, trying to understand why. Sometimes I think Freud should have left well enough alone.

July is going out in a blaze of glory—*my* glory! Oh, future daughters-in-law, I have sorely betrayed you. I have, for the first time in my life, *baked my own bread.*

I don't think I could have received wilder acclaim around here if I had swum Bering Strait. My ego is blossoming accordingly. I feel like a goddess. But come to think of it, I'll never lose ten pounds if I bake my own bread.

I feel like an *overweight* goddess.

AUGUST

I DON'T KNOW how it got to be August. It seems to me it was just February yesterday, and here I am plunging on and still wondering if this is a book. Will it prove I can write, or just that I can *type?* If you gave a chimpanzee a typewriter and taught him how to type—or her, let's make it her, a housewife-chimpanzee—do you suppose *she* could write a book? I don't know, but there are times it would be handy to have a nice chimpanzee to type up a couple of pages for me while I whisk around and get the dust out of the corners.

August. Well, in August I'm so busy planning for September that I hardly notice the month at all. It's a kind of nothing month, anyway; the kids are sick to the teeth of vacation but won't admit it, and I'm sick to the teeth of the kids and am glad to admit it, every ten minutes. It's not our kids; I could stand just our kids, a mere measly half dozen. It's all the kids in the neighborhood, milling about like a mob scene from a biblical production by Cecil B. De Mille. The yard is so full of bicycles and stray toys of every description that we ought to put up a sign: ACME JUNKYARD—WE BUY, SELL, SWAP ANYTHING.

The house—never mind the house. You've heard the old saying, Cleanliness is next to Impossible? It was written by somebody with six kids.

Life has, moreover, been more disorganized than usual around here because Wayne slipped a disk while wrestling rocks around in the rockery the other day. The doctor has been by, ordering bed-rest, hot baths, and the hot-water bottle, plus 292's for the pain. But there are no pills to counteract the idiocy of a man who thinks the best way to rotate a boulder into position is to flip it in mid-air and catch it coming down. He caught it, all right, the same way he caught it the last time he tried doing it that way.

The sight of somebody lying on a bed in the middle of the day unnerves me. I don't think I ever went through a period in my little-girlhood when I wanted to be a nurse. I knew myself too well, even then.

Nothing else gets written, except this. I am spending every spare minute peeling apples for the flood of applesauce with which I am slowly and inexorably drowning the family. I expect them to build an ark and load into it and leave me behind any day now. We have gone through two tins of cinnamon. However, I feel very creative when I bake a batch of bread, and more than that, I feel virtuous and useful at the moment, having caught an error in the galleys of Wayne's latest paper, after both he and the editor of the journal had already checked them.

Postcards have been arriving from various points along the Alcan Highway, followed by a letter. My sister Lois and her husband and four children have been driving to Alaska and are now on their way back; they are going to stop with us for a couple of days to recuperate from this harrowing experience. It seems it rained all the time and if there was any scenery they couldn't see it anyway and the highway was bumpy and the car has had overdrive trouble and carburetor trouble, and if they hadn't told everyone they were going to Alaska, they'd have turned around long ago and gone back home.

Our children are excited at the prospect of a cousinly visit, such being rare, and are preparing entertainment. They are busy in the rec room, constructing a set and rehearsing. Horrible noises rise up through the furnace vents, somewhat like the sound effects for *Donovan's Brain*. What they are going to do, they tell me, is to present "The Creation of Frankenstein's Monster." They have Duncan's ultraviolet master science lab kit, with make-up paint that glows after exposure to his ultraviolet lamp, and they have arranged on a table a marvelous Rube Goldbergian arrangement of test tubes, beakers, bottles, rubber tubing, and so forth. Duncan has borrowed my white cotton summer jacket for Dr. Frankenstein's lab coat. He, naturally, will be Dr. F.

When I was eleven or twelve I used to put on magic lantern shows in the basement for the neighborhood children, but I never had siblings my own age to cooperate in such a marvelous theatrical as this promises to be. Suddenly I find myself remembering the dramas produced by Jo, Beth, Amy and what was the name of the other March girl? Meg, of course. . . . I just ran upstairs and found the book, my own old one, and (oh, self-indulgence!) have been sitting here reading my favorite chapter, "Under the Umbrella." And do you know something? I believe that all my life I must have wanted to marry a bearded professor. I always wept when Mr. Bhaer asked Jo, "Heart's dearest, why do you cry?" and she answered, "Because you are going away," and if the first time I read the book I thought Laurie romantic, it was all swept away when the end of the book drew near and I met Professor Bhaer. That's because I'm Jo, of course. Well, I have my bearded professor now, although I had to marry him young and unbearded and wait seventeen years for the beard to show up. What a wonderful feeling to discover that I have, all unawares, realized one of my early ambitions! And I am, I think, as happy as Jo herself. . . .

And as poor, too, at the moment. I am counting pennies from now until the 18th of the month when the Family Allowance arrives (our consolation prize for having children). We have $4.16 in one bank account, $3.26 in another, and $25 in a third. And August is always the month in which all the clothes left over from the last school year suddenly fall into tatters from the rigors of summer wear. Everybody needs new shoes by the first week of August but I try to postpone the purchases until the last week of August, hoping to send them to school in shoes that look just a little bit new. I have made a school-clothes shopping list and added up the probable cost, starting with six pairs of shoes, four pairs of corduroy trousers, a nice school dress, and sweaters. Let us not even dwell upon the shabby edges of the professorial suit of clothes.

We have been trudging about the house finding fault with it, too—the shabby upholstery, the couch covered with a homemade slipcover of charcoal cloth generously overlaid with dog and cat fur, the big bookcase loaded two layers deep with books (any book I ever want is in the behind layer). The sheaf of unpaid bills in my desk drawer has outgrown one paper clip and I've sorted it into two sheaves, urgent and slightly less urgent. Who drew that lovely cartoon of the family gathered round while Dad—eyes shut or blindfolded—reaches into an overflowing hatful of bills to discover who is to be the lucky creditor this month?

I typed a paper for Wayne and thought he'd get it mailed off today, but instead he is spending the entire day on three footnotes.

Duncan has been upstairs making a long list of Meccano construction parts and checking it against a catalogue. There are piles of Meccano parts all over the floor of his room, along with little boxes and jars of nuts, bolts, and other small bits. It looks to me as if he has enough to build almost anything, in the original size. Some of this Meccano was birthday and Christmas loot, but the major portion of it and the reason for this meticulous inventory is a recent acquisition through barter. He tells me he now has $79 worth of Meccano, list price, of course.

Meccano is nice, but $79 worth of Meccano, spread all over the floor so I haven't been able to sweep up there for three days—well, it reminds me of the woman whose husband sent her to a psychiatrist because, as she told him, "I like pancakes." "Good grief," said the psychiatrist, "what's wrong with that? *I* like pancakes, too." "Oh, good!" cried the woman. "Then you must come see mine —I have *trunks full!*" Just what is going to be done with all this Meccano I don't know—but I can sure guess.

As a woman who not long ago spent two solid afternoons stirring pots of simmering dye on the top of the range, turning old pillowslips into jet-black capes and old blue jeans into suitably sooty trousers to match, and rinsing the lot in tubful after tubful of water while my hands turned a pale grayish purple, I know whereof I speak. Living with six children is not so difficult; it is living with their brief but furious enthusiasms that provides the real test. A parent must live not only with Junior and Sis, but with model airplanes and button collections, with Davy Crockett, Elvis Presley, and with Zorro.

Moderation is a quality unknown to childhood. At least no child of mine possesses it. My children are so immoderate that I have learned to think twice before proposing any activity or hobby to fill an empty hour. The question I have to ask myself is, to what extreme can this thing be carried—and *am I prepared for it?*

I wasn't really prepared, for example, when on our trip to Mexico a doting friend in California presented the boys with a few matchfolders and I lightly suggested they might collect them from the places we visited. From then on, from San Francisco to Ensenada and back home again, three of the four boys raced ahead of us into every restaurant, pounced upon the matchfolders next to the cash register and then rushed wildly through the door marked MEN, not for the usual reason small boys rush through such doors, but to see if some traveler had thoughtfully left a folder therein. This was mild enough, but I had to learn to look the other way while they snagged them from the floor and from the sidewalk, or walked up to an aunt they hadn't seen in five years and asked "Gotny matchfolders?" before she had barely begun to straighten out which boy was which. After all, *I* had suggested it.

During the same trip Mac, who collects rocks, attempted to bring back the entire state of California with him, piece by piece, in the station wagon. He was really in operation when we visited the lava flow area of Oregon—such huge chunks were so light and portable! If the wagon had not already been crammed with agates and jasper and fossils and seashells, he would have managed to cart home enough lava to build up a small volcano of his own. This is why all my sheets and towels and pillowslips are crammed into one small corner of the linen cupboard, and if the state of Oregon ever has a strange feeling that something is missing, now they'll know where to come to get it.

I still remember when we got Duncan a small Brownie box camera and he took his first roll of slightly slanting pictures. Now he has a 35-mm camera with filters, portrait lenses and a half dozen other attachments, a basement full of gadgets, dozens of bottles of chemicals and packets of paper, and a $120 enlarger with a color head. Days go by during which the basement windows are boarded up with heavy cardboard, the water runs at a steady drizzle into his washing trays all evening, and you can hear him down there chanting "One-thousand-and-one, one-thousand-and-two, one-thousand-and-three—" Then he comes roaring up the stairs full blast to set my oven timer so that it will signal the end of yet another of the complicated steps of color printing. *Nobody* can go down to the basement for a hammer or a screwdriver or a game of ping-pong without his permission. Of course a hobby like photography is bound to make a person more aware of the world about him—like, for example, when we rode on the Skyway cars in Disneyland and he was in the little car behind me. "How did you like it?" I asked, when he got out at the other end. "I don't know," he said, "I was changing the film in my camera."

I've learned that when you teach a child to bake you have to eat chocolate cake every night for three solid weeks (and appreciatively!); that when you laugh at a funny remark you have to laugh at it several times a day for days on end; that when you assist one child in turning himself into a television character, you will soon have to dye old pillowslips for four or five children, some of them not even your own; that a boy who is praised for putting together a little $5 transistor radio kit will shortly have the house full of wires, tubes, resistors, transistors, speakers, and assorted screws, nuts, bolts, wire cutters, screwdrivers, drills, and things for which you will not even have names, will hound and harass you until you relent and agree that a homemade radio is exactly what you want for your birthday, and will go off in a corner and sulk because you call a repairman instead of letting him fix the television set when Maverick splits into three pieces and looks like a Nude Descending a Staircase.

But the hard part comes later. It comes when you see the equipment gathering dust in the basement, the match-folders consigned to the wastebasket, the camera with Christmas pictures still trapped in it in mid-July. It comes when the weathervane turns unnoticed in the back garden and no small boy rushes out each morning to read the velocity and analyze the cloud formations and enter it all in his notebook. It comes with that sad moment when you find the black capes and trousers kicked into a corner, and you get them neatly laundered and present them to all the junior Don Diegos, and they—they refuse them politely. "Aren't you going night-riding any more?" you ask. "Nope," they say, "Zorro's out of season."

If Love and Hope are eternal, so are plasticene and color crayons.

New toys are beautiful, bright and shiny, but nothing is nicer than an old toy that many children have loved. All their love gets tangled up in the matted plush of an aged Teddy bear, from whence it radiates until it is hard to tell whether the child is loving the toy or the toy the child. Old Teddy bears and old Raggedy Anns are the best of loved and loving toys, more absorbing of love and more giving. I found Polly not long ago weeping over our old Raggedy Ann "because I'd forgotten about her!" she sobbed, and we took Raggedy and laundered and ironed her dress and her pinafore, and colored in her faded features a bit with red pencil and a little ink. We still have the Teddy bears the big boys had when they were small, and a little knitted kitten that brought a look of such transported joy to Malcolm's face nine years ago, I think the light from that smile is still traveling somewhere, in space. I think of all these things because I was just dusting a little rocking chair, a chair of oak and real leather and of precisely the right size, which used to be mine when I was a little girl of four or five; and I have been hoping that it will still be around for our grandchildren to rock in. I can still sit in it, to watch television, but I have to be careful when I get up or it gets up with me.

Something you might guess about me from all this: I *hate* teen-age dolls with bosoms and bras and girdles and nylons and high-heeled shoes and mink stoles. They are as cuddly and loving as a pair of scissors.

The cousins are here—my sister, her husband, three girls, one boy, and one medium-large part-beagle dog named Bosco! Excuse me for a couple of days, please.

My sister, to her youngest girl, aged twelve: "Pamela, have you brushed your teeth?"

Pamela, on her way out the back door: "Well—al*most!*"

I am still trying to work that one out.

We have had a wonderful time. We put up our tent and their tent (which needed drying) and cousin Benjamin's private pup tent, and did a ton of laundry full of Alaskan dirt. The children found a vacant lot full of ripe blackberries—three pies and still some left for berries with cream and sugar. We spent hours over cups of coffee and more hours over sinks full of dirty dishes and it took two rooms and three tables to hold us when we ate.

"I like Joanie best," whispered Jill, "because her face is all freckles"—like Jill's face, of course.

At one point I counted sixteen children playing a wild game of guns in the back yard, and there were three or four more inside. The carnival aspect of the place with three tents pitched under the trees must have attracted well over half a dozen neighborhood children. I looked out, counting and holding my reverberating head, and one of them looked up at me and cried, with a grin and a wink, "Never mind, we'll be gone in three or four hours!"

But the high point of the visit was, easily, the production of "The Creation of Frankenstein's Monster" in the rec room. The audience was ushered into the totally dark room and led singly, sidling, down a narrow passage past the "set" to the seats beyond. Darkness—silence—a few nervous titters—then a match is struck, and Dr. Frankenstein is revealed in his laboratory, lighting a candle under a beaker of something or other. Before us, lying on a table and completely shrouded by a sheet, is a body. Dr. Frankenstein putters with his equipment, mutters to himself, calls in his assistants (Karkov and Zharkov, if I remember correctly), and the play begins. There is much scurrying out and fetching of liver, kidneys (my sister and brother-in-law are strangling with suppressed laughter), blood, and a nice fresh brain (the wrong one, of course, as per script), while hideous electronic noises issue from the equipment of the sound man. In the final analysis it was hard to decide whether the play's real climax was the moment at the end when the candle went out and the Monster, his painted face glowing in ghastly colors in the dark, rose from the table and advanced on the cowering audience, or the moment when the "blood" being transfused suddenly boiled over and splattered the whole set, or perhaps the moment when Dr. Frankenstein leaned carelessly over the candle and his lab coat caught fire. Well, that wasn't much of a summer jacket anyway, and I might as well be philosophical about it and be glad Dr. Frankenstein didn't go up in flames (and the rec room and the trapped audience with him).

I think Duncan is a little put out because the play turned out to be such a howling success—as a comedy.

Gastronomic adventure: we have finally got around to trying those canned toasted baby bees from Japan, and have discovered that they make ideal nibbling with a glass of beer. The children have all bravely tried them too, Jill saying, with a shudder, "*You* pick one up and put it in my mouth, and *then* I'll eat it!" It's an interesting idea, being able to eat something you can't bear to pick up.

Why is it Malcolm will gladly eat toasted baby bees when he won't eat spaghetti, lasagna, meat loaf, fried onions, gravy, curry, stew, and any casserole you can name except plain macaroni and cheese? And how can a boy hate strawberry shortcake and love *broccoli?* Hate baked beans and love *Brussels sprouts?* Hate mayonnaise and love *artichokes?*

CHEERS! HUZZAHS! CARTWHEELS! HANDSPRINGS! SIGHS OF RELIEF!

The editors of *Redbook* have bought a story for $850! Thumbing through my card file, I can report that I wrote and first mailed out that story *seven* years ago. Every editor in New York must have turned it down. Isn't there an adage to the effect that if you keep something for seven years you'll find a use for it?

All that lovely money—I dream of school clothes, and shoes, and socks, and money in the bank for Wayne's trip to Mexico City, and the elimination of those two bulging paper clips full of bills. My mind runs over rapid calculations: $850 minus 10 per cent for my agent is $765, which will shrink further when turned from American into Canadian dollars but I am too delirious to care.

I may love old battered Teddy bears but I also love new fresh money. And if I love this old battered house and the rather ungracious life we lead in it, that isn't to say that there aren't some mornings I wish I could get up, put on a filmy peignoir, step out on my balcony overlooking the Mediterranean, and ring for breakfast on a tray. Right now I've got all of last year's boots and rubbers lined up in the kitchen for the children to try on so I'll know who needs new ones. Not a job for a lady in a filmy peignoir. Oh well.

We have been talking about getting a piano. (No, I haven't bought a new vacuum cleaner yet.) We've wanted one for ages. Of course all I can play is "The Pagan Love Song" and the first three bars of "Anitra's Dance," but let's not let a little thing like that stop us. I had seven lessons once, before they foreclosed the mortgage, so whether or not I have any talent is a problem that has not yet been explored. We have several musical instruments: an accordion which Mac and Andy have both had a few lessons on, a guitar the boys gave Wayne for Father's Day a few years ago and which he hasn't learned to play yet, a recorder, a harmonica, a shakuhachi (a large Japanese bamboo instrument which rivals bagpipes in its unwillingness to part with the music that must be trapped inside it somewhere), and a stringless banjo. I can play "Sweet Betsy from Pike" on the accordion and, sometimes, "Home, Home on the Range." But "Home on the Range" somehow fails to satisfy me when what I really want to be able to rip off is Bach's Toccata and Fugue.

Well, a man's reach should always exceed his grasp, they say.

My favorite instrument is actually the clarinet, but I've held one in my hands only once in my life and then I couldn't extract a noise from it. It was a great disappointment to me. Thinking about it makes me sad.

Duncan has baked his first lemon meringue pie. I should hate to have my first lemon meringue pie come floating up out of the past for comparison. Floating? It would have to be scraped up and *dragged* in.

There is nothing effeminate about Duncan's interest in cookery. His cooking has, I think, a double impetus stemming from (1) his large, omnivorous appetite and (2) his passion for messing around, a sort of chemical interest. He is a sloppy chemist and a sloppy cook, always fishing bits of eggshell up out of the whites (or catching himself on fire when creating Monsters?), but he bakes a terrific chocolate cake, better than mine. Someday some girl will marry a physicist or a mathematician and discover she has also married a chef—but she had better be prepared to stand by with a broom, a mop, and a damp cloth.

We have broken the back of the back-to-school shopping and I must report that the boys took longer to choose their one new shirt apiece than Polly took to select a dress and a cardigan. My check for the *Redbook* story hasn't arrived yet, but I can charge things merrily with the knowledge that I can pay the bill by the time it arrives. Wayne has gone to do some research in the Provincial Archives, and I am contemplating cleaning the house before school begins—and also, just incidentally, before my mother-in-law and sister-in-law arrive for a visit next week. Meanwhile Malcolm has reaped his just rewards for digging on cold winter days with the university archaeology club. He has gone upriver with one of the students to the summer dig, the first time he has gotten out from under the parental thumb without being put under the thumb of the Y.M.C.A. or the Junior Forest Wardens. The invitation came suddenly and he left the same afternoon, half delirious with delight. It seems very quiet and depopulated here with only six of us about.

Something on television last night got Duncan started on one of his marathon conversations about man, the universe, atomic physics, et cetera, and at one point he launched into a favorite topic: Man the Cosmic Accident. "What makes us think we're such examples of survival of the fittest, anyway?" he asked. "Look at the ant—is three-quarters of the world's ant population starving?" I finally put the lid on him at midnight, but with difficulty.

This reminds me of some thoughts I've been mulling over recently concerning children and television.

Our children have been watching assorted forms of violence for several years now, ever since we let those men walk into the living room with that box full of gun-toting cowboys, private eyes, and psychopathic characters in large, imperfectly lighted, drafty mansions. We don't watch anything near the number of TV hours reported for the average family, but still the first sentence Jill ever spoke was "This is the CBC."

We didn't deliberately offer up our kids for an experiment on the effects of TV violence upon the normal child; it was more laziness than anything else. But now that the experiment is well under way I feel it necessary to make a preliminary report. What brings me to this decision is that I found myself, the other night, telling the boys that there was "something good on at nine." What is it? they asked, with the usual suspicion of children who expect it will be a filmed visit of two dear kiddies to a Holland dike. "A murder," I said cheerfully.

A moment later when my own words came back at me like a boomerang, I tried to worm out of a deluge of self-accusations. Well, I argued silently with myself, grownups like a good murder and, after all, what are kids but little grownups who haven't grown up yet? But this didn't seem to make too much sense, and I was forced to sit down and think it all over carefully.

They are, more or less, normal kids. At any rate, they *seem* to be normal. They quarrel incessantly, they eat constantly but not at mealtimes, their allowances are never big enough and neither are their clothes, they despise work and are convinced that the touch of a washcloth on the human neck is certain death. (These, of course, are their negative aspects; they are also sweet, thoughtful, helpful, loving, et cetera, et cetera, and I wouldn't give you one for a million dollars even at the exact moment I'd like to sink them all in the river with a large bag of stones.)

We do exercise a mild kind of censorship, mostly editing out trash rather than violence per se. (Let's face it: a lot of good stories are pretty violent!) I turn off the set when the reception is bad or when I find them watching their third cowboy show in a row or when they become hypnotized by a succession of aged Betty Boop cartoons. I have a personal aversion to Howdy Doody and I'm afraid I'd turn it off even if the children didn't agree with me; however, they find it just as nauseating as I do, so Howdy Doody Time is always time to turn off the set or find another channel. There are, generally speaking, no late movies for the boys on school nights and only one a week even on nonschool nights, that one chosen from the listings with a heavy parental veto in readiness. "But it's a *classic!*" is Duncan's war cry; and in a dispute, the classic usually wins out. If Shakespeare came on at 2 A.M. I'd probably wake them up to watch. (Shakespeare has his grisly aspects, however. When Polly was four and Cameron was seven, they watched *Hamlet* on two successive afternoons and twice within six months, and at that time one of their favorite games was to go out in the garden and dig Ophelia's grave. Polly, being fair and wistful of face, fancied herself as Ophelia. Luckily, Cameron never thought to carry the burying out in actual fact.) Nevertheless, they have seen all kinds of violence in the past few years, for I am addicted to murders, spy stories, even Boris Karloff in the late movie, and we all adore Alfred Hitchcock.

Some people who pooh-pooh the effects of TV violence upon the child have asserted that the child does not absorb the stuff, that it goes right in one ear and out the other (and into the eyes and out the back of the head, I suppose). I think people like that are dead wrong. Children don't let *anything* go in one ear and out the other, not even commercials. (Mine can recite them all.) They don't even let parental commands go in one ear and out the other; it just looks that way. You can test the truth of this by eavesdropping on any group of children who are playing at being parents. "I've told you ten times to pick this jacket up off the rug!" they shriek at each other, and, "You children are driving me *out of my mind!*" The accuracy of their mimicry is shattering.

I know that our children, at least, think about the programs they watch. I know because I have been trapped in the occasional, interminable, post-TV bull sessions in which they hash them over. That body on the living-room floor with the knife quivering realistically in its back—they remember it all right, and the more talented ones (like Malcolm) may practice staggering about and dying for our edification. But what they seem to be really and genuinely concerned about is the problem of a dishonest district attorney, or the possibility of a prejudiced jury, or the injustices of vigilante action. The details of the crime are momentarily engrossing, but what engages their minds afterwards are the moral dilemmas and the problems of good and evil.

This is true in our house. It may not be true in any other house. How it came to be I don't know except that we are a very talky family, and there is a limit to how long you can talk about that quivering knife but no limit to how long you can talk about morals and ethics. And even a rather poor TV murder show can give parents a chance to guide a good discussion.

I've left the girls out of this, of course. They are too young to watch television later than seven-thirty or eight at night, with an occasional exception for Shirley Temple Storybook or something special on the Ed Sullivan Show. But I've noticed something interesting about them and TV violence, too. Although most cowboy dramas bore them, they can watch without seeming to be in the least troubled; Jill, in fact, watches everything with an air of casual indifference. Polly, however (and remember, she is the older one, turned seven this month), frequently runs squealing from the room, unable to bear what is happening before her eyes on the TV screen. Is it murder? Is it horror? Is the fire burning down the old homestead with Mary and the kids trapped inside while the Indians dance about with hideously painted faces? No, it's Lucy in some ridiculous scrape or other, or Beaver Cleaver has lost some money down the gutter or broken the car window or let the bathtub run over. *That's* when she cries "I can't stand it!" and runs for the kitchen to wait until the tense moment passes.

Mac is back, full of stories of being ferried across the river in a small boat at night and hiking three miles to the dig, part of the way through a railway tunnel full of rats—what a glorious adventure for a twelve-year-old boy!—and having his first train ride part of the way home. He is already begging to be allowed to join the dig for a while next summer ("if they ask me") and hardly dares believe me when I say "Why, yes, of course." He has the natural skepticism of the child, assuming that it is very unlikely that a parent would want for him the very thing he so desperately wants himself.

And Wayne is back, too, as delighted in his own way. No daredevil boat rides nor hikes through rat-infested tunnels, no great scholarly discovery in the archives either, but at a furniture store he bought a curious piece of carving which seemed strangely familiar to him and which the proprietor was glad to part with for the sum of $5. After a hasty thumbing of our battered copy of *Arts of the South Seas,* it turns out to be a breast ornament from Easter Island, and worth at least five or ten times what he paid for it.

August draws to a close, pulling summer after it. I remember the summers of my young-girlhood—but not golden enchanted days of heat and languor, not an old swimming hole, none of that. What I remember is an all-pervading sense of desolation and loneliness on those days when everybody else seemed to have gone somewhere, everybody but me, and the only shouts and laughter I heard were blocks and blocks away, and the only children around were either too young or too old. My sisters, who were ten and twelve years older than I (a difference that is small now but was a vast, unclosable gap then) were like two aunts instead of sisters, and September couldn't come soon enough to please me.

In this crowded, noisy, bulging house, these children of ours won't have to experience that kind of loneliness.

Should I envy—or pity—them?

SEPTEMBER

I LIKE September, and not just because the children are going back to school; I liked it even when I was a child and I was the one who was going back to school. I think I like September because after three months of that aimless season, summer, I am anxious to get back to work.

It's come over me lately that I don't much like having fun. In fact, I don't even like the word "fun." It depresses me, like the word "laff"—you know, as in a Hollywood comedy advertised (usually erroneously) as a Laff Riot. The words "laff riot" are absolutely guaranteed to turn me away from a theater faster than a two-block-long queue in a rainstorm. But I've had my eye on this word "fun" and I think it's gotten out of bounds.

Now, I'm not one to use the dictionary for a final authority. Speech has to keep transgressing dictionary boundaries; it's in the nature of things. Of course, sometimes the results are fairly dismal—I'll never get used to being told to "tissue off" the cleansing cream from my face, but I suppose anything simpler and more Anglo-Saxon sounds just too vulgar for the beauty industry.

"Fun" has become an adjective. "Make it a fun holiday," says the magazine writer; or, "Redecorating your living room can be a fun project;" or even, in the words of one of my friends addicted to this adjectival extension, "I had a fun evening" and "He's a fun person." My husband has pointed out to me that there is a tendency in English to widen the use of monosyllabic words. Monosyllables are phonetically stronger: try substituting the word "enjoyment" or the word "pleasure" in the phrase "Are you having any fun?" and you'll see what I mean. And as a phonetically strong word becomes overused and overextended, it grows semantically weak—it means so many things that it means almost nothing. Think of the word "nice," which once upon a time meant foolish, or silly, and then affected, coy, or shy, and now—well, as Mammy Yokum says, "Good is better than evil because it's nicer!"

It's possible that "enjoyable," "pleasurable," and "satisfying" are just too long as words; but it is also possible that just as a laff with two f's is somehow different from a laugh with a u-g-h, "fun" somehow means something less than enjoyable, less than pleasurable, less than satisfying —something, I suspect, less lasting and more superficial. Whatever it is, leave me out; I don't want any.

Fun has nothing to do with funny, of course. No one is asking you to reap humorous results when redecorating your living room as a fun project. What they mean, I suppose, is that you should live it up, serve shish-kebab to your fun friends, divide yourselves into fun teams, wear painting caps and fun smocks inscribed with fun slogans, and see which wall gets painted first—a fun game, obviously. This is the kind of thing I refuse to do. If I want to paint a wall, I want everybody to go away and let me paint; they can take their fun friends off and have their fun somewhere else, also their shish-kebab.

I don't know why painting a wall has to be fun. Or why anything has to be fun—or everything, for that matter. When I paint a wall, I expect to paint a wall, getting a certain amount of solid, sober satisfaction out of it. The terrible thing, actually, is that *I like work.* I get kind of a bang out of work. But I don't intend to start saying Work is Fun, like some Orwellian character in *1984* insisting that Slave is Free, and so on. What I want to know is, what is wrong with work that we have to make fun out of it?

Some time ago, in the *Journal of Social Issues,* there was an article called "The Emergence of Fun Morality" by the psychologist Martha Wolfenstein. I was led to read the article by a quotation from it in a magazine I was leafing. The quotation described a child's arithmetic book written in cowboy terms, with all the problems involving cowhands and horses, et cetera. Miss Wolfenstein commented that she didn't know whether this made arithmetic any more interesting, but she did have a suspicion that it made cowboys less exciting.

I've always wondered why learning has to be transformed into fun. I had a Latin teacher once who loved to make Latin into fun, but I spent so much time making a working model of Mt. Vesuvius that I missed the whole subjunctive mode and had an awful time with my final examination. In my own dogged, gloomy way I enjoy mastering a set of facts and have always hoped that my children might be led to find the same sort of enjoyment. It seems like a better approach to learning, if only because it is more lasting. I don't know what happens to the little cowhand who gallops through his range-riding arithmetic and then comes face to face with differential calculus. Perhaps some clever college professor of mathematics can write a textbook of differential calculus in cowboy terms—but I doubt it.

I don't even understand why learning has to be made painless, because at least to me the pain of learning something difficult is strangely exhilarating, like the painful exertions of mountain climbing or of running a race. Doing something difficult and challenging always entails effort; it may even entail discomfort, and it may not be fun at all. But I'd hate to go through life without it.

Back to fun morality and Miss Wolfenstein, who pursued an interesting line of research. What she did was to analyze the approach to child rearing as given in United States government Child Care handbooks over the past forty years or so. To put it as briefly as possible, forty years ago pleasures were inherently dangerous, and a child's impulses toward such dangerous pleasures as thumb-sucking had to be curbed. A mother worked at being a mother; she was diligent, vigilant, and tireless, mostly and especially in her unceasing efforts to keep the baby from doing what he wanted to do. Forty years later the baby's impulses are seen as harmless; what he wants he may possibly need, and what he wants and needs is doubtless good for him. Formerly the mother was warned against playing with the baby; now she is encouraged to enjoy him. Thus play and fun have gradually been divested of puritanical associations of wickedness.

Which is all to the good. But wait. Now something new enters in—the word "should" and the word "ought." Mother should enjoy her baby, baby's bath should be fun, feeding ought to be fun—and if it isn't, then something is wrong. The mother who doesn't find taking care of her baby a continuous laff riot is not only missing a lot of fun, but probably has some deep-seated psychological difficulty (like not enjoying being waked up at 2 A.M., maybe). Perhaps this isn't so dangerous if you are merely considering babies; babies are, after all, fairly amusing little animals most of the time, except when dirty, wet, hungry, and at 2 A.M. But let's leave baby care and proceed, with Miss Wolfenstein, to a more general consideration of this Fatally Urgent Neurosis, *fun*.

Once upon a time, Miss Wolfenstein points out, work and play were isolated. Virtue was associated with one and the danger of sin with the other. Now, however, the two are so intertwined that both have become diluted and diffused. Not only that, but when you don't have fun there is something wrong with you. Even at play we keep asking ourselves if we are having as much fun—that is, doing as well—as we ought to. Having fun has become a kind of obligation, and those who fail at it are made to feel guilty, ashamed, inadequate and miserable.

I don't know just what people like me are supposed to do. I've made a kind of life career out of *not* learning to play bridge, and I added to it a few years ago the sideline of *not* learning to play canasta. I have also avoided ping-pong (or table tennis, as its serious devotees insist), social drinking of any proportions, the rumba, the tango, the mambo, and the cha-cha-cha, movies with Jerry Lewis, and bowling. Don't tell me I don't know what I'm missing. I know what I'm missing—a lot of fun. And if not having fun is something to be ashamed of, not even wanting to have fun must be ten times worse. It's bad enough to say wistfully that you never seem to be having any fun, but to admit brassily that you don't give a hang whether you have fun or not, and that given your choice you would rather sit in a corner and work than whoop it up with a lot of fun friends at a fun barbecue—well, that's enough to start all the fun addicts jotting down for you their psychiatrists' phone numbers. (Fun numbers?)

I get to feeling kind of depressed about this. It seems to me that this kind of thing is taking all the fun out of fun. But Miss Wolfenstein thinks she can see the faint beginnings of a change; perhaps fun morality will eventually go the way of mah-jongg and miniature golf. Perhaps if I bury my head in my work deep enough nobody will notice what a depraved, inadequate, fun-hating sort of character I am; and when I come up again maybe people will be enjoying themselves again instead of going around worried sick over whether they're having enough fun.

Which is why I like September, the beginning of the busy season.

I packed up half a dozen short stories a couple of weeks ago and mailed them to the CBC for a new short-story reading program. They've come back now, minus one which they're buying. Of the other five, they'd like to see two again, one of them padded to size, the other cut. I sat down immediately and hacked away at the one they wanted cut, but by the time it got down to size there was no story left, so I put it back in the filing cabinet. Then I took the one that needed padding and have been carefully plumping my little story out in all the right places, putting in three hundred extra words. I can't remember ever having to do this sort of thing; before this it's always been cut, cut, cut. I have to admit that there seems to me something unethical and sneaky about sticking in these extra words, like winning a beauty contest while wearing falsies.

Every year in June the kids come home from school with a free ticket each to Children's Day at the Exhibition, and since the Exhibition (a fall fair, complete with rodeo, circus, and a gayway) doesn't roll around until the last week of August and the first week of September, I squirrel these tickets away in the front of my 3 x 5 card file and save them there all summer. In late August the Exhibition begins with a huge parade, which some of the children go downtown to see while the rest stay home with me and watch it on television. I try not to choke up and weep at every big brassy band that goes by, and it is a little easier when it's only television and not the real thing. Besides, 80 per cent of my attention is focused on trying to pick out the rest of our kids in the crowds lining the streets. Last year I saw them very plainly, sitting on a fence, but this year all I got was a headless view of Malcolm. I knew it was Malcolm not only from his jacket but from the patches on the knees of his trousers—I'd know those patches anywhere.

I almost thought I might go to the Exhibition myself this year, but I turned out to be as chickenhearted as usual and stayed home. The boys went once by themselves and again when Wayne took them along with his nephew Dean. Everybody reported that it was "real neat"; nobody got sick, nobody wasted more money than he could bear to waste on the games, and nobody rode upside down on anything and dropped all the rest of his money out of his pockets (which is what Andy did the year before), so it sounds like an unqualified success this time. Duncan is busy turning part of that $79 worth of Meccano into a giant model Ferris wheel which he is hooking up to an electric motor so it will really work. And now, just as I'm at the point of deciding (after cleaning, shopping, cooking, cleaning, cooking, shopping) that the only way to write a book about the family is to observe them fondly for a year and then shoot them before sitting down to write it, I find myself gazing in tranquil rapture at the calendar—School Starts Tomorrow!

By the time night school starts at the end of the month there will be eight of us shooting off in six different directions to six different schools: the university, the high school I'll teach at, the high school Duncan will go to, the junior high school, the grade school, and the little private kindergarten Jill will attend. And I, for the first time in over thirteen years, will be alone in the house for regular, specified, daily hours—to wit, 9 A.M. to noon. The prospect of all that treasure of silence is almost frightening. Will I spend it properly? What if I waste it? Oh, just to sit quietly and stare into space and daydream for three hours without having to wipe a nose, bandage a knee, settle a quarrel, hand out cookies, or say, even once, "Pick it up" or "Shut it" or "No!" Even that sounds like a recipe for living to be one hundred—to which I aspire.

The first day of school—and Duncan is back already. Despite my shrieked warnings about not losing any lists or anything, he managed to dispose of his program on the way home and has had to go out again and search for it along the way he came. He has the habit of stuffing his pockets full of a number of things and then pulling out a Kleenex with complete disregard for whatever may come with it; I have even seen dollar bills float insouciantly to the floor, despite his passionate concern for money, of which he never has enough. Jill is registered in kindergarten; she pointed out to me, shyly, this morning, where her name was already printed on her locker. Kindergarten is just at the end of our block, no streets to cross, no transportation problem—who could ask for anything more?

Duncan (back with his program, which he found on the street) informs me that there is no place at the high school to park bicycles. I check with my friend across the street, who has put three boys through high school already, and she informs me that nobody but nobody rides a bike to high school. If you don't have a car, you ride a bus. If you don't ride the bus, you walk. On the first day of school, she says, a few freshmen not in the know show up on their bicycles; then they go home and put their bicycles in the basement or the garage and that's the end of it. Riding a bicycle to high school simply Isn't Done.

Duncan, however, is aghast at the idea of 14 cents a day for bus fare (so am I) and equally alarmed at the prospect of hauling eight or more textbooks and a huge zipper binder a dozen blocks on foot each morning. "Well, *I'm* riding *my* bike," he says grimly.

Another lesson in nonconformity.

When all the educationists deplore the increased use of cars among the high school students, it seems peculiar for them to play right along with it by failing to provide even one little bike rack for those few hardy individualists among the crowd.

Duncan points out that even if he wanted to drive a car he wouldn't be old enough to have a license until a scant six months before he'll be due to graduate from high school anyway.

"They'll laugh at him," my friend warns me.

"Let them," Duncan growls.

The corn ripens but it obviously isn't going to amount

to much this year. I don't know why we grow it, as a matter of fact. It takes up a tremendous amount of room and if we added up all the corn we'd probably find we were getting only a few dollars' worth. But it's so pretty when it grows, and there's something so satisfying about going out into the garden and picking your own corn, so I suppose we shall go on growing it, regardless. Next to the corn, the pumpkins are beginning to turn yellow. The garden is full of robins energetically hunting for worms and bugs.

Wayne has a new suit, an Irish tweed in which, with his beard, he looks remarkably like Peter Ustinov, large and somewhat shaggy. I like it.

No sooner do we get our hands on some money than we find some new place to get rid of it. This time it's the announcement of the International Darwin Centennial Celebration to be held at the end of November in Chicago. I have sat with the budget, figuring and juggling, until I am fairly certain Wayne can manage that trip as well as the Mexico City one without undue financial disaster. He doesn't quite believe me but is willing to take my word for it—anything rather than look at the figures himself, for if there's anything he hates it's arithmetic. Sometimes this frustrates me, when I battle all alone with the intractable columns of Income and Outgo (never the twain shall meet), but mostly I am glad, glad, glad. Nothing could be nicer than a husband who can't even remember the amount of his annual salary and has never done more with his income-tax return than to sign it when I hand it to him, all filled out. I count how much money he takes with him when he goes on a trip, and count how much he brings back, and enter the difference in the budget.

Once in a while I ask him what he spent today, especially if he's been to the hardware store; but mostly I just wait until the end of the month and subtract what I've spent from the amount that has obviously dribbled through our fingers and the difference must be what *he* has spent. This keeps him more or less happily uninvolved with the whole issue of money, which, I gather, is what he prefers.

A most astonishing thing has happened. I, to whom the word "shortstop" means something you dip snapshots into in the darkroom, have a favorite baseball team! I, for whom the words "foul ball" conjure up visions of a dismal dance, have a favorite pitcher! I, one of the leading anti-baseball fans of the century, have discovered Henry Wiggen and the N.Y. Mammoths. I sing their praises to the skies. I do a little jig of joy. As it happens, the N.Y. Mammoths are a figment of the imagination of an author called Henry Wiggen; and Henry Wiggen happens to be a figment of the imagination of an author called Mark Harris. I just phoned a downtown bookstore and ordered a copy of his latest book, *Wake Up, Stupid,* and I shall be watching for the mailman.

I began by reading *Something About a Soldier,* which wasn't about baseball but mentioned somewhere on the dust jacket or environs that this writer Harris had written a couple or three books about a baseball team. Having read *Something About a Soldier* all in one delighted gulp, I narrowed my steely eyes and said, All right, you, let's see if you can make me read a book about a baseball team.

He can.

I went to the library and got out *Bang the Drum Slowly* and sat in bed and wouldn't turn out the light until it was finished. The next day I sent a child to the library to bring home *A Ticket for a Seamstitch* and I sat in bed and read *that* one until it was finished, and now I am wondering why we have such a lousy library because I am trying to get my northpaw on *The Southpaw* but they don't even have it.

I refuse to try to tell you what it is about Mark Harris's writing that I like because I am not quite sure what it is, myself. But any man who can make me read a book about a baseball team has obviously got *something.*

My quiet mornings are heavenly. I just do the dishes, sweep up the Cheerios and Alpha-Bits and cornflakes from the floor, bring the typewriter into the kitchen nook, and sit down. I can feel that shriveled little dried pea of Just Me expanding inside the layers of Housewife, Mother, Cook, Laundress, and Accountant. Just sitting here and looking out into the garden refreshes my squashed and weary soul. Jill trots off to kindergarten by herself, and comes back at noon; and I think that somehow that experience refreshes her, too, for she seems to be able to spend the afternoon quietly amusing herself at the kitchen table with crayons and paste and scissors. I whisk around doing the rest of the housework in my minimal fashion, and one day a week we go up to the supermarket and perhaps the library.

But I still have eczema. I refuse to believe that it's because I can't make up my mind whether to leave my husband or not, as Dr. Alvarez suggests in the newspaper column, although I suspect that if I don't get rid of it soon *he* may make up his mind to leave *me.* It's only a little patch as big as a half dollar on my palm, but by the time I've sprung a leak in my third pair of rubber gloves in two weeks and am fuming and muttering and cursing and smearing everything in the house on my hand to no avail, it would seem more as if I had a galloping case of some kind of hideous tropical blight. The doctor has prescribed cortisone, and I have a new little jar from the drugstore—what looks to be about two teaspoonfuls for $2.65. After one day's application all I have to say about it is that what previously *itched* now *hurts*, and if that's progress I'm not very much satisfied with it.

I have just baked four loaves of bread and a cake with a 7-minute icing. This is to take the family's mind off the fact that dinner is mostly leftovers.

It's a beautiful day. Everything is turning red and gold, and one house on our way to the store is covered with scarlet Virginia creeper. I am reminded of cold wintry days when I was ten or twelve and the leaves had all fallen from the vines on our brick chimney and I went outside to tear them down in the afternoon twilight. They were long and sinewy; I whipped them around and around in the air above my head and they whistled wonderfully. There are still some leaves from that vine pressed between the pages of some of my books—leaves at least a quarter of a century old.

I am typing while watching the robins and cedar waxwings gobble the dogwood seeds outside the window; across the garden I can see the largest of the pumpkins turning orange at the edge of the corn patch. The dogwood, however, is confused in its seasons. I think it has grown so old that its system of communication has broken down, for it has seeds on one branch and flowers on another. Like a senile human being, it has yesterday and today and spring and fall and past and present all muddled up.

Yesterday Mr. D. reached through the fence and took a cucumber; Wayne saw him and told me. The cucumbers are old and huge and horribly bitter, and what he wanted it for we couldn't imagine. But later, when Wayne was out in the garden, he came to the fence and confessed, explaining that he'd wanted it to dry for the seeds. A small theft, considering the baskets of peaches Mrs. D. sets across on *our* side of the fence when their little peach tree is overloaded.

A lot of people feel rotten after a hearty breakfast. "Refreshed" does *not* rhyme with "best" unless you've been putting rum in your Coke. Parents should shout at their children from time to time if they feel like it. Making a big fuss over Negro entertainers doesn't help the race relations problem. Drinking vodka may help ease cold-war tensions, but I doubt it. A person gets his most refreshing sleep not before midnight but in that ten minutes after the alarm goes off in the morning.

Duncan is still riding his bike to school every day. "Who else is?" I ask him.

"Nobody."

Maybe my eczema will vanish when I finish this book. On the other hand, maybe it is just all my internal cussedness breaking out. I am a very trying woman, you know. I once threw a plate of pickled beets at my husband. I don't remember why. I didn't hit him, either; I hit a friend instead.

Wayne and I have had quarrels. We have had disagreements and troubles a lot more serious than the flinging of a plate of pickled beets. But we just don't belong to the class of people who rush off to the divorce courts every time things go temporarily sour. ("Judge, she threw a plate of pickled beets at me!") And we have survived.

Love has a lot to do with it, love that is compounded

of tenderness, sex, tolerance, exasperation, understanding, and an agreement about life.

But another thing that has a lot to do with it is talk. The first time we ever went out together we sat on my mother's front porch until three in the morning, talking, talking. We began talking that first night and we talked through succeeding dates on succeeding nights until it became apparent that we could spend our whole lives talking to each other without becoming bored. Now, after eighteen years, we still like to sneak away for a drive or a walk together, so that we can talk without interruption.

I think we got married so we could continue that first conversation of ours.

My night-school class in Creative Writing begins tomorrow night. I am torn between wishing for a good class full of people with some talent or for less than fifteen people to show up so the whole thing will be canceled. I don't mind leaving the house two nights a week before the dinner dishes are done, not at all. But when I get back at 10 P.M. and the boys jump up guiltily from in front of the television set (having forgotten their homework entirely) and the girls' clothes are strewn all over the downstairs as if they'd done a perambulatory strip tease, and the kitchen, after several snacks, looks just as if dinner had just been finished—then's when I wonder why I do it. I start picking up things before I even get my coat off, and Wayne comes wandering in to greet me with a book in his hand. He just hasn't the temperament to be a Constant Nagger.

Table conversation with our children is not what is recommended in books on manners. We have tried to draw the line at medical matters; and Duncan used to ask each time we had meat, what part of the animal is this and what does it *do?*—which is easier to answer with steak than with liver and kidneys. We finally clamped down on that conversational gambit, but we still get discussions of the symptoms of various poisons and what happens if you get exposed to lye, acids, gases, etc., etc. A favorite table topic is, of course, *food,* but not "The Most Memorable Meal I Ever Ate." No, Malcolm discusses eating liver and beets, because Duncan loathes them; and Duncan expounds on the joys of spaghetti and buttermilk, Malcolm's and Andy's pet hates. When this palls (my contribution having been mainly, "Elbows down, boys," and "One hand is enough, Duncan," and "Eat it, Malcolm"), they begin a program of shoving each other, making horrid noises, feeling each other's muscles, and so on. Jill picks the items she doesn't like from her plate and passes them around to the rest of the family, dropping them unceremoniously on plates. Somebody spills the milk, somebody else drops a whole boiled carrot—this, oddly enough, is always somebody who hates carrots—and Mac carelessly leaves his napkin covering half his plate as he excuses himself from the table; but I am not so stupid, for I pick it up and find a little heap of rice and green peas, and he has to come back again. Duncan, who despite his hatred of liver and beets puts away considerable food at each sitting, surveys the table with despair and comments on the wastage. "Some people who are starving in China would be glad to have this," he says gloomily. But this eloquent mention of the world's famine-ridden population fails to move any forks. I begin to clean plates, eating the things I cannot bear to throw out, wishing our dog and cat were a bit more omnivorous than they are. As long as I do the dishes, there is no hope of losing that ten pounds. I eat another entire meal just piling things up by the sink.

And the next night what do they discuss at the table? The Battle of Thermopylae.

Out in the night, a train whistles. Never mind jet planes or rockets to the moon, the sound of a train whistle in the night still makes a lovely prickle up the back of my neck.

Suddenly I remember certain long cross-country bus rides, and what it is like to be dumped, sleepy and aching, into a little coffee shop at midnight in some unknown little town. You drink coffee and eat a doughnut, feeling as if you have wandered into the middle of a painting by Edward Hopper, and you eye the clock and find the toilet and finally crawl back aboard to go roaring off again on a dark highway somewhere in the middle of America. I am never more patriotic than at such a moment.

I have a class, some twenty of them. One man paid for the course by peeling a fifty from a wad of bills too big for a billfold; I think he had it rolled up and held together with a rubber band. I made $30 change after stuffing my eyeballs back into their sockets. Does he expect to have *talent*, too? At the end of the session a woman, wearing a fringed leather jacket, told me she would have to miss the next session as she was going to a convention in California. A convention of what? I asked. "Doberman Pinschers," she answered.

Dog stories, I thought.

OCTOBER

OCTOBER makes me think of octagons and octogenarians and octets, which is an unfortunate thing because I always have to count on my fingers to figure out that it's really the tenth month and not the eighth. I don't have that trouble with September because I never think of septagons or septuagenarians or septets; and November, really the eleventh month and not the ninth, is easier to straighten out in my mind because it's so close to the end, which is December and not the tenth month but the twelfth. Maybe if we just threw out February, which I would never miss, and one of those useless summer months along with it, we could get the whole thing squared around so that my smattering of Latin would come in handy again.

October also makes me think of colors: gold and blue. Gold leaves against a flawless blue sky, the whole world gold and blue and a crisp day ending with a fine sunset. I have never become reconciled to rain in October; it doesn't fit in with my idea of the month.

By October we have gotten into the swing of the fall and winter season. Homework is in full flood; nightly the battle rages over the long kitchen table, and I stand guard to make certain nobody strays near the television set until all his assignments are done. Duncan, Malcolm, and Andy, who are in high school and junior high and loaded with work, rage and fume as Polly and Cameron, the grade-schoolers, lightly underline a few words in a workbook, add a few columns of figures, and dash off to the living room and freedom; *they* sit drawing diagrams of Bessemer furnaces, mumbling declensions of Latin nouns, writing "A Letter to Khrushchev and Eisenhower," committing chemical formulae to memory, and kicking each other under the table. Every morning the children count off the days until Halloween, and the usual annual quarrel about firecrackers and fireworks begins to boil. I am, meanwhile, counting the days until Christmas and contemplating the three birthdays that will arrive between now and then, including two in December—bad planning, obviously. I begin to make lists.

I am sitting here in the kitchen nook, surrounded by wads of crumpled yellow paper, a bouquet of withering pansies (we still have pansies in October), a cup of coffee dregs, and the morning mail. Outside the window—which needs washing—a group of little greenish finches flick about the dogwood branches, eating seeds. A gleam of yellow pumpkin is visible through the branches of the apple tree. The sun is shining. A silence so deep spreads over the house that I call out "Jill?" and getting no answer I go to investigate and find her asleep on the living-room rug, her head on a pile of bright-colored building blocks. I move her to the couch and cover her with a sweater and look at the clock. It is 3:20 and the silence will soon be broken with repeated openings and slammings of the door as the other children arrive home from school. I put the kettle on for tea, which the children drink diluted with an almost equal quantity of milk.

A use has been found for the old, dissected vacuum cleaner. Andy is making the pipe extensions into rockets. He can't—thank goodness—expect to launch them, but at least they look more impressive than the ones he's been making out of old ball-point pens: Every time he tries to fire one of *those,* it melts.

Anything airborne fascinates Andy. His little closet-room is papered with pictures of airplanes, rockets, satellites, and missiles; he makes one airplane after another, undeterred by one crackup after another, and he can stand forever at the end of a control line watching a plane go around and around and around with the blankly sober, hypnotized expression of a three-year-old on a small merry-go-round. This passion is of at least five years' standing and after five years I have stopped waiting for something else to supplant it. For Andy, it will be *Ad astra* . . .

Duncan, on the other hand, is brooding over plans for a home-built Van de Graaf generator which he can buy for $79—a mere $79. "When will you be able to lend me some money?" he asks. I give him a long Jack Benny stare.

Harry Golden reports his disappointment in discovering that the Israelis have no sense of humor. I could have warned him, even though I've never been there. Any young, self-consciously nationalistic and superpatriotic nation full of people dressed in khaki and young girls marching around with rifles is *bound* not to have a sense of humor. I'd never have expected a sense of humor. It took 3,000 years of persecution to develop that marvelous and peculiarly Jewish sense of humor and then it can be lost in one generation in Israel.

Thank heaven we still have plenty of Jews left in America. I think I have always been a Jew at heart. A kind of crypto-Jew, perhaps. It isn't because I love sour cream, either. I was uninformed enough to wonder where the butter was for my bread when I landed in Beth Israel Hospital once; it was a meat meal. Nor do I love all Jews automatically, any more than I love all Negroes, all dentists, or all Presbyterians. Maybe it's just that once in a while I think of what the United States would be like if all its Jews and what they have contributed were removed, and it makes me shudder.

Mac asks me if he can be campaign manager for somebody named Pat Underhill in the school elections. The idea of Mac's willingly undertaking a job such as this, knowing full well he will have to make a speech in the auditorium, astonishes me. Yes, of course, I say, trying to visualize this new, socially more courageous Malcolm.

Duncan was somebody's campaign manager a year or two ago, but that didn't surprise me. He has always been fearless on the public platform, and upstairs in the little girls' closet there still hangs a blue percale Little Boy Blue costume he wore during the Spring Program of the first grade, years ago. We had sat through the whispered, barely audible contributions of several children, and then the curtains parted again to reveal a large plywood book labeled "Mother Goose." The cover opened and out stepped Duncan; he strode to the center of the stage, blew a loud blast on his horn (covered with gold florist's paper), and said, "GOOD AFTERNOON, FRIENDS. I AM LITTLE BOY BLUE!" in a voice that rocked the parents in their seats and made me double over, convulsed with laughter and tears at the same time. I have been on the point of throwing out that costume half a dozen times since, but the memory of that moment stops my hand and I hang it up again.

There are still nasturtiums, marigolds, snapdragons, and roses in the garden, but the leaves are falling and some of the plants are beginning to look brown and autumnal. Canadian Thanksgiving will be here soon (I still struggle yearly with the concept of a Thanksgiving that arrives before Halloween) and the school Fall Fair, and a big faculty tea at the new Faculty Club.

Nothing is nicer than a little girl singing cheerfully around the house. But when she comes closer, I hear Jill's song: "Great green gobs of gooey, gooey, gopher guts . . ."

Suddenly our three-year fire-insurance policy has fallen due. Why didn't somebody warn me? Not only that, but it, like everything else, has gone up, so that I am trying to wedge it into the budget and still leave room for that trip to Chicago. But who knows, maybe I'll sell another short story. I cross my fingers, and remember that my luck always works best when I'm out on a limb.

Unforgettable sentence from a student story. Our hero is getting into a cab. " 'To the Palms Hotel,' he said, satirically."

The same student had two men in a cocktail bar behaving "in an incipient manner."

I suggest, gently, a dictionary.

I read aloud to the class, for our first plunge into class criticism, a student story on the Mau-Mau troubles. One gentleman, carried away by the opportunity, launched into a long critical attack, prefacing it with the remark that the author had obviously never been in Africa. I let him finish, but I couldn't help informing them all that the author—a young hyphenated Englishman whose hair constantly falls into his eyes in approved English fashion—had spent two years on the Kenya police. I don't mean to dampen their critical fires, however; it is usually too difficult to get them going. One would think all of them were relatives and friends of each author in turn, and it takes vigorous pokings with the instructor's stick (figuratively speaking, although at times I wish I *had* one) to stir up a little action.

Sometimes I ride to school on the bus with a little old lady who is taking Russian on Thursday nights. I had been admiring her, dauntless soul, for tackling a new language with such spirit; but last night she told me she had to meet a friend at the corner, to help her up the two blocks to the high school building. "She can't see very well," she said, "and really she oughtn't to be studying Russian, for she has to hold the book right up to her face to make it out; but she's so keen on it, and she visited Russia last year . . ." I walked along with her to the corner, and there waited her friend: a bent, tremulous old woman whose most exhausting activity one would suppose to be watering her house plants and feeding her cat. And there she is, studying Russian at high school every Thursday!

Every time I think of her I smile with delight at the triumph of the human spirit.

I love talking to people on buses. But an enormous

percentage of people who ride on buses are (1) engrossed in deep philosophical thought of their own, (2) afflicted with a muscular spasm of the neck muscles which causes the head to turn automatically away from the nearest person, or (3) scared to death.

The easiest people to talk to are the bus drivers themselves. Of course it says PLEASE DO NOT TALK TO THE OPERATOR right up there in the front of the bus; but where I get on, all the buses have a ten-minute stopover, and I'm usually the first and only passenger. If I arrive ahead of time I can get in a little talking before we start.

I don't know why I like talking to strangers so much. Maybe it's because all during childhood I was warned against talking to strangers and now I can do it with impunity. But by talking I mean about 30 per cent *talking* and 70 per cent *listening,* because I'm a kind of curious, snoopy creature.

Mac is working on his "campain speach" (I see the words written on the back of his sheet of paper) and only now do I discover that Pat Underhill is Patricia and not Patrick. Hmmm.

We have celebrated Thanksgiving. We went to San Juan Island to visit Nana and Dada, and, forewarned about the opening of hunting season, we were prepared to leave our station wagon parked for the weekend near the dock. Hunters' cars were lined up well back into town; one affluent quartet had chartered a small bus, which was filled with their gear—we could see them inside, playing cards. There was no point attempting any walks in the woods during our stay. The first morning I woke at 5 A.M. to the roar of hunters' automobiles racing up the town's one main street, and in the distance as soon as dawn came up we could hear the intermittent sounds of gunfire. It was a soggy, drizzly weekend anyway, and we contented ourselves with walking around town, playing interminable games of cards, and watching television.

Despite the fact that deer are so plentiful as to be a constant pest in the San Juan Islands, I am always rooting for the deer and not the hunters. But my sentiment does not extend to the dinner table. I will eat venison if you serve it to me.

Every time we go anywhere in the car we are on the road only five minutes before Duncan wants to know, "Who wants to play Twenty Questions?" The answer is usually *nobody*, and Duncan begins to fret. We have driven the road to the Anacortes ferry dozens of times, but I am content to watch the scenery go by; there is always something new, and each season is different. But Duncan is bored. "Why don't you just daydream?" Wayne asks him. Duncan's reply is scornful: "I'm not *schizophrenic!*" he says.

My mother-in-law has the most beautiful bird-feeding station I have ever seen. It is a large, wooden structure, resembling nothing so much as a wayside shrine of some sort, beautifully carved and painted white, blue, yellow and brown, with a little St. Francis of driftwood in the back. It's new and no birds have come yet, but when they do I foresee some protracted mealtimes—it is right outside the window by the dining table.

But if there's anything I'd rather watch than birds, it's fish. Our aquaria are better than Equanil; doctors should prescribe fish-watching for nervous patients. Sometimes, to calm down, I simply go into the study and sit down on a large footlocker (doubling as footstool and coffee table) and watch. There is a tank full of Cameron's swordtails, another tank with Sylvie the goldfish—a beautiful white creature with elegantly graceful fins and tail—and some sticklebacks, and a third tank with tiny catfish wiggling about, twitching their ferocious Fu Manchu "whiskers." In a fourth tank Pender the painted turtle is beginning to slow down, eating very little, and thinking of hibernating.

I didn't go to the Fall Fair but I did go to the tea at the Faculty Club. As for the former affair, the children brought home two brown teapots, a carving knife, some silver-plate casserole holders, and assorted other small wares from the White Elephant sale, and Malcolm won an angel-food cake in the Cake Walk. This is the first year I haven't scurried around to find something to send. Maybe it's just as well—Duncan, hunting for twopenny bargains, might have bought it back again to bring home.

The Faculty Tea was highly overpopulated. We searched rather frantically for people we know—they were searching for us too, and one of my friends insisted that the entire faculty had probably been changed over the summer and only we had been overlooked, through some administrative oversight. The impression was hard to escape. Eight years here and all I saw was a room full of strangers.

I *don't* like to talk to strangers at *teas*. Buses are another matter entirely.

The best part of the whole tea was the millinery. I went hatless, as usual, and stared unashamedly at all the hats. There were some real lollapaloozas, worn by women with dishonest mirrors.

I've been trying to figure out how much money I've made writing so far this year. It's a microscopic sum. Why don't I pay somebody to keep house for me, write twice as much, and make scads of money? Well, I've *tried*—don't think I haven't tried—but I've discovered that there must be some women who are psychologically incapable of letting someone keep house for them, no matter how wretchedly they do the job themselves, and I'm one of them. Part-time housework and part-time writing suit me best; I have to push a broom awhile to be glad to sit down at the typewriter and I have to pound the typewriter for a while to be glad to get up and push a broom. I may not do either splendidly, but I have to do both—or else move to a hotel.

It would be a different story were I ruthless and driven by feverish aspirations—but who can be ruthless with a 4-year-old girl leaning on her knee and saying. "Mommy, you know what? I like you, Mommy. I love you . . . bigger . . . bigger than this whole house!" And I lose the thread of my paragraph and sit for a while with Jill in my lap, rocking back and forth and whispering silly endearments: "Jill, you know what? You're sweeter than 17,825 little black kittens with white feet and their whiskers dipped in cream!"

Do I have any aspirations larger than this—larger than this house, this small reputation, this miniature career, this circumscribed life? I do, of course, and maybe it's all my deferred aspirations that are giving me eczema. Someday the poems will get written, someday the Broadway play, someday the Big Novel that frightens me more than a little. Someday, even, the Book I Am Supposed to Be Writing!

For now, I play around at it, serving an apprenticeship with words, ready to stop and bake chocolate chip cookies or pack five school lunches or press a Junior Forest Warden shirt. Ruthlessness is for spinsters and bachelors, not for me.

And from a mere mother I have leaped to being a grandmother—of sorts, that is. Gordon phoned to tell me that Virginia has had a baby girl, Peggy Ann, and all's well. The hospital informed me that only parents and husbands are allowed in Maternity, but Wayne and I decided we qualified and were prepared to argue our status; but, we didn't meet any opposition anyway. A hospital regulation is only as good as the number of people available to enforce it, and whoever heard of an overstaffed hospital these days? We just walked in.

Wayne says he doesn't feel particularly grandfatherly. Whether I feel grandmotherly or not I don't know; how does a grandmother feel? Maybe later, when I'm a "real" grandmother, I'll know. It seems to me there must be a vast difference between a grandmother's feelings about a baby born to a daughter and her feelings about a baby born to a daughter-in-law. Later, I suppose, one regards the children with equal grandparently love (as equal as any love is, and that's another question), but at least at the moment of childbearing it must be different to have the daughter you've borne bear her own child. There, remarked Wayne (always the anthropologist), is a factor that would bolster a matriarchal society; and upon deeper consideration, it is rather difficult to see how patriarchy ever got started.

Never mind theory. The facts are that Virginia looked happy and the baby looked cute and I must go shopping for a nice blanket and some diapers, which are what they need. There's also that big box of outgrown baby things in the linen closet upstairs; I knew there was some reason for not giving it to the Salvation Army last time I started throwing things out.

I came home from school the other night and discovered that Cameron had decided that we ought to give a Halloween party. I had suggested it as a substitute for (1) firecrackers and (2) those huge bags full of gooey trick-or-treat candy. (Why, one year Duncan's hoard lasted until *Easter!*) Outside the front door Cam had posted a blackboard reading, HALLOWEEN PARTY, COME ONE COME ALL, STAY FOR DINNER. I had a load of books under one arm, but I picked up the board with the other and hastily brought it in. "Whaddya mean, 'come one come all, stay for dinner'?" I shrieked. "Well . . ." said Cam, in an injured voice, and I could see I was being thoroughly unreasonable even though there are at least ten boys on our block between the ages of 10 and 14 not counting ours.

But the issue is settled now. A Halloween party, but with an invitation list, and *after* dinner. I'm a hard woman.

I showed my good intentions by buying a dozen orange Halloween balloons when I shopped for groceries. Cameron wanted to blow them up right away, of course—more than a week in advance!

I think I must, after all, be secretly envious of Wayne's various journeys-in-prospect, for I dreamed last night that it was I who was having correspondence with somebody in Vienna, not he. It seemed they wanted to publish my book there (when I dream I really go off the deep end!) and I was to take a trip there and discuss it. However, the entire correspondence seemed to be in an outlandishly bizarre and ornate German script and I couldn't make head nor tail of it. I woke up completely frustrated.

You know something? People are too darned apologetic about dreams. Most people nowadays tell you a dream with a kind of furtive, timorous, sheepish enthusiasm, as if they were giving you a birthday present they knew they hadn't spent enough money on. And other people assure you that they never dream at all; they are usually very proud of this, and very arrogant. Only simple-minded people, they imply, have dreams.

Now, I like dreams. I've had funny dreams, beautiful dreams, terrifying dreams, melancholy dreams, perplexing dreams—but never a dull dream. My only regret about dreams is that I can't always wake up carefully enough to remember them. You've got to be cagey about the way you wake up if you have any interest in dreams. Too often I have waked with a start and there's a little figure by my bed and a little voice saying, "Mommy, I'm wet!" And confronted with cold, hard—wet—reality, the dream goes slithering away like a weasel through a fence, and I'm face to face with damp pajamas and frozen orange juice and five-minute porridge and another day. I've lost a lot of good dreams that way.

I don't know why people have become so apologetic about dreams. We weren't always that way. And there are still some places left in the world where people regularly tell their dreams, mull them over, discuss them, and generally get their money's worth out of them. Places other than a psychoanalyst's couch, I mean.

There are various ways of approaching dreams and dreaming. There is, of course, the standard meaning-of-dreams method. Every society has its own lore about what dreams mean, and generally a great part of this is concerned with what dreams can tell you about the future. There is divination by dreams, or oneiromancy—which is a word fascinating enough to repay one for merely thinking about dreams. But actually, because it becomes so cut and dried—you can get little handbooks of dream interpretation with lists and lists of meanings—this can turn into an awful bore.

There is also Sigmund Freud. Now, I have no great quarrel with the Freudian interpretation of dreams. Or at least my quarrel with it has nothing to do with its validity as a psychoanalytic method. All I maintain here is that it's a sure-shot way to spoil a rattling good dream. And it's also one good reason why people have become so timid about telling their dreams. There is nothing more unsettling than telling a dream and then spying among the faces of your audience that one smug little smile that belongs to the person who has a line on Freudian dream interpretation. It's enough to put you off dreaming for a month.

I don't like those approaches to dreaming at all. They're too destructive. What I like is a perfectly naïve, uncomplicated, romantic, impressionable enthusiasm—I call it the Mystery Tour Approach. What I mean is this: when you go to bed at night it's just like buying a ticket for one of those mystery-tour bus rides—five hours of going somewhere and nobody knows where, not even the driver, until he opens his sealed orders. Prepare yourself to enjoy what comes, and off we go.

The Freudian analysts who dissect dreams are concerned with the way in which dreams reveal and reflect reality. What I prefer to be concerned with is the reality of the dream itself. Not that I don't occasionally pick at a dream later and wonder why the man sitting on top of the church tower turned out to be my old professor of social psychology—but I don't do much more than that. What I like is the dream itself as an experience, for a dream *is* an experience. When you dream you are in an Egyptian tomb you are *in an Egyptian tomb* even if it straightway turns into the New York subway; it is quite different from sitting fully awake and trying to imagine you are in an Egyptian tomb. It is only the rare and highly imaginative person, the real poet, who can actually enter the Egyptian tomb while still awake. But when you are asleep and dreaming, the things that happen to you *do* happen to you; and though you do not experience them with your body you experience them with some part of the mind that registers and records things as having been experienced. And that is, after all, the one thing that makes dreaming the wonderful and terrible thing it is.

(Have you ever tried to face, the next day, a perfectly casual acquaintance whom you kissed in a dream the previous night?)

I'm sorry for people who don't get anything out of a night's dreaming. It's a dreadful waste, really. As for me, I've had some beauties. In fact, some of my dreams are more real to me than things that have really happened, and there are dreams I remember far more clearly than any number of waking experiences. I dreamed once of walking into a strange, desolate building set in a wasteland that Salvador Dali could have painted. I found myself in a room that was a morgue, with shrouded bodies on tables everywhere I looked. I turned the covers down one by one, and looked at face after face, and then I turned and looked into a mirror—and I too was dead. I dreamed that dream eighteen or more years ago, and it might have been last night, I remember it so clearly. I dreamed once, during the Spanish Civil War, that I was machine-gunned from a Madrid window and lay in the gutter, dying in the hot Spanish sun. But I also dreamed a comical dream, that I had married a bear, just like a girl in a fairy tale. I've dreamed of wandering in strange cities, of climbing alpine paths and seeing vistas of incomparable mountains and great chasms at my feet where fogs and clouds swirled. I've dreamed the usual dreams of leaden legs, ringing schoolbells and vain struggles with a load of huge books; I've dreamed of Oriental bazaars, riotous with silks and brocades all mine for the asking. Dreams pleasant and unpleasant, some downright grisly, some as chilling and inventive as a story by Edgar Allan Poe. Once, searching wildly in a dirty attic, filled with terror, not knowing what I wanted or even who I was, I found a scrap of newspaper *dated a thousand years from now.* I woke shuddering, gripped with horror.

If you are of the Freudian persuasion, may you enjoy musing over the revealing data of my nocturnal imagination. But don't tell me; I don't want to know. I prefer my dreams just as they are: mystery tours, adventures unlimited —until morning.

Andy made some remark at dinner last night about "Mac's girl friend." "WHOSE WHAT?" I asked. "Mac's girl friend—Pat Underhill," Andy said.

Now I know why Mac has been polishing his shoes every second morning.

Malcolm and Cameron have been decorating the rec room for the party. (Andy and Duncan are remaining aloof, but just wait until the time is upon them; I am used to this.) There are skulls and crossbones and a skeleton, cats and witches and pumpkins, and Cameron has cut out dozens of tiny pumpkins of orange paper and pinned them to the dark-brown curtains at the rec-room windows. The four big pumpkins from our pumpkin patch have been brought in to await carving, and are down in the fruit cellar. I must bake brownies and buy ice cream and wrap prizes for the games.

The party notwithstanding, the controversy about firecrackers still rages. "Just a few, to shoot off at the end of the party?" they wheedle, and against our better judgment we relent, knowing that all the other children in the neighborhood will have won the same argument as they do every year. Secretly—no, *openly!*—we hope that the P.T.A. succeeds in getting the things outlawed once and for all next year.

A firecracker accident, like death, can never happen to *you,* only to somebody else. The newspapers fill up with accounts of lost fingers and injured eyes, but our children believe themselves to be immune.

Cameron still wants to blow up the balloons. "After dinner, right before the party," I tell him. He is crushed, even though he knows full well how balloons shrivel and shrink. "*Okay,*" he says, unhappily.

We have been invited to cocktails a week from Halloween. I wish cocktails could be abolished right along with firecrackers, but there will be people there I get to see about three times a year (due to laziness on all our parts, of course) and I am looking forward to it. I would look forward to it a bit more if I thought I could zip up my last year's cocktail dress without giving up oxygen for two hours. Naturally I have forgotten all about dieting. A string on my finger wouldn't help; what I really need is adhesive tape across my mouth.

I am sitting up waiting for Wayne to come home after a late lecture engagement; not out of any wifely devotion or concern, mind you, but because he promised to bring me—*a rat trap.*

In the middle of last night I heard a rustling in the kitchen. Drat that dog, I thought, what's she into now? But when I padded into the dark kitchen, I realized the sound came from high on the kitchen cupboard—and I knew Muff, our cat, was outside. It was too much noise for even a bevy of mice (What do mice come in? If it's a *pride* of lions, is it a *humility* of mice?), and I went back into the bedroom to wake Wayne. He came (grudgingly) and turned on the light, whereupon a middle-sized black rat slithered down and skittered around the corner into the bedroom. "In the bedroom!" I cried, and Wayne charged in. The rat turned and charged out, and promptly vanished into the hall and was seen no more. Wayne, in fact, didn't see it at all and had to take my word for its existence; but my reputation was saved by indisputable rat-tooth gougings in a quarter pound of oleomargarine sitting on a saucer. (With a shiver, we consigned it to the garbage.) But Mr. Rat was gone, and we had to go back to bed and try to get to sleep.

Do you know something? I was once animal caretaker at the Radiation Laboratories at the University of California. I have handled hundreds of rats—white, black, and parti-colored—but when Wayne turned on that kitchen light I jumped up on a bench and stayed there. Why, I even had a half interest in a pet rat once; her name was Ludmila Pavlichenko. She was coal black and we often gave her the run of the house, but she was a dainty laboratory rat, and that makes all the difference in the world. This was the first time in my life I ever saw a rat (except for Ludmila) running around inside a house.

Brrr!

Here comes Wayne—ah, he has the trap! Other men bring their wives orchids, and chocolates, and jewels. Mine brings a rat trap.

If having a rat makes us a trifle déclassé, never mind—we once had maggots in the diaper pail. I was typing Wayne's Ph.D. dissertation at the time, day in and day out, night in and night out. (There are certain songs that will linger forever in my memory with a peculiar nostalgia—the ones the all-night disk jockeys were playing that spring.) Toward the end I stopped for nothing, absolutely nothing. I finished typing 45 minutes before the deadline for Ph.D. degrees for that term, and Wayne went sprinting to the campus with all 521 pages of the thing. After a heavy sigh of relief, I looked about the wreckage of the house and decided to begin with the accumulated diapers (Cameron's, then). I opened the slightly askew lid of the diaper pail, recoiled in horror, and then—well, what else could I do?—began to laugh hysterically. I had no washing machine and had to do the grisly things by hand, but I was still laughing—and washing—when Wayne got back.

It's the sharing of deep emotional experiences like that that bind a marriage together.

I was nearly twenty-one before I ever saw a cockroach, and I had to go to New York's Lower East Side to see *that*. The only cockroach I'd known before that was archy—and Kafka's, in *Metamorphosis*, of course. The first real cockroach I saw, in fact, was perfectly white, and stone dead. Not an albino, no, but a sample of the decorative genius and money-saving talents of New York landlords. The apartment I was inspecting was advertised as newly decorated to account for the incredible rent; and indeed it was. Several rooms had been painted, practically yesterday, an almost blinding white. Everything had been painted—walls, baseboards, pipes, blisters of old paint, dirt on the windowsills, and a dead cockroach in the kitchen corner.

Late at night, October 31: The Halloween party was one of those all-too-rare magnificent successes which bear, I think, a very slight relationship to the amount of invested effort. It didn't seem as if we had done much, but the rec room was resplendent. The ping-pong table was covered with an orange cloth, held down by two huge jack-o'-lanterns and one small one in the middle, the walls were adorned with witches, cats, pumpkins, and Mr. Bones, and a great cluster of orange balloons hung from the ceiling. The children were also resplendent in their costumes; guests arrived as beatniks, gypsy ladies, robots (in cardboard cartons), and a green devil. Cameron had spent his entire allowance on a skeleton costume, but the others saved their cash and improvised. Jill came as a scarecrow in a souvenir hat from Ensenada and a mask manufactured by brother Cam. Polly was an Oriental in kimono, zori, slanted-eye make-up, and a hat made of an old photo flood-lamp reflector, Andy was dressed in two yellow bath towels imprinted with leopard spots in black pastel crayon, carrying a huge driftwood club, Mac had a machete, a basketry hat, some barbaric jewelry, and a doll's head which he carried by the hair—a head-hunter, of course. Duncan (who raced around at the last minute, moaning about having no costume—an annual Halloween performance of his) was in a wig of matted, hair-thin wire from his radio junk and a sport coat two sizes too small (not hard to find), as one of the Three Stooges. All in all, a memorable affair. I felt like Elsa Maxwell.

The trap was sprung this morning, but no rat. However, when we went to fetch the pumpkins to carve, we discovered that friend rat had been at one of them, so we left it there and reset the trap next to it on the floor of the fruit cellar. We'll get him yet.

Farewell, October. We are going to bed.

NOVEMBER

THE FIRST sound we hear in November is the desultory pop . . . bang . . . fzzzz-sput . . . pop-poppoppop of the firecrackers which were lost, mislaid, or misfired the night before and are now being harvested by little boys who have slipped out of the house before breakfast. Gleefully they pick over all the bits of red that litter the street. Pop! Bang! We turn over in bed, but I, unlike Wayne, don't have a slightly deaf ear to turn up. Bang! Fzzzz! Sput! POP! No wonder scientists and military men are conspiring to blow us all to Kingdom Come; imagine the thrill of setting off one of those big firecrackers down at Cape Canaveral.

We had other excitement this morning, too. Down in

the fruit cellar, next to the gnawed-on pumpkin, our rat lay with his nose in the trap. Everybody had to inspect him first, and then he was buried. No—before he was buried he had to be measured (seven inches of body and nine inches of tail) and he had to be properly identified according to "Smaller Mammals of North America" (Nelson, the *National Geographic Magazine* for May, 1918) and *Mammals of Washington State* by Dalquest. He proved to be, Wayne informed me (with some pride), a *Rattus rattus rattus*, a black rat, and not a *Rattus norvegicus*, infinitely more common and also infinitely uglier. The Norway rat, I learned, is the grayish, yellow-toothed, sneering rat, fierce and numerous and clever, that quickly comes to dominate any area in which it lives, driving into obscurity and sometimes extinction the black rat, a much prettier creature with sleek fur and a daintier air. Ours (we have already begun referring to the creature with pardonable affection) was really a handsome fellow; and we realize now that he wasn't even living in our house, not really. No doubt someone left the basement door open and he must have wandered in. He probably would have been glad to get out again, what with all the noise we make and that wretched trap. Poor *Rattus rattus rattus*; I am sorry we could not coexist.

There are, I think, very few members of the animal kingdom for which I have a really strong aversion. Mice, in the wild, startle me with their sudden dartings and scurryings, but I have had pet mice and I have a particular love for the strain of laboratory animals known as Bar Harbor mice. Flies I dislike for purely sanitary reasons; I don't care to get stung by bees and wasps nor bitten by mosquitoes, but I don't react violently to their mere presence. Spiders are another matter. I like daddy longlegs and there is nothing lovelier than a dew-hung spiderweb—out in the woods or hung on a fence, where it belongs. A big, fat, hairy spider walking across my living-room floor, however, gives me the shivers, and I can't imagine having a pet spider, though I have heard of such. Nevertheless, I have cared for a pet snake, a fine two-foot bull snake named Oscar, who loved nothing better than to coil around your arm and rest his head on your shoulder. He never gave me the shivers. It is a practical business to be wary of rattlesnakes, and in any strange place a strange snake would be something I'd avoid. But there is only one snake that fills me with horror. I can watch huge pythons and bone-crushing boa constrictors (all behind glass in a herpetarium, of course) and regard them with due respect for their powers, but when the cobra rises up and draws back and spreads its hood, my temperature drops 20° and my vertebrae rattle like Spanish castanets. I don't even like those little rubber ones—you know, you press a bulb and the air pressure makes the snake come up out of the basket?

A snake has no business standing up like that. It's unnatural.

Never mind the poem that goes "no sun, no something, no something-else, No-vember"; I like November. I like the quiet, drifting, gray and foggy peacefulness of November, the occasional bright days with the last few leaves falling, the days that move imperceptibly from morning to night without a shift in color or light. November is like the room I imagine I should have to write in, a small, cool, gray, quiet, plain room—a cell, perhaps, a monk's cell. November is a kind of optimum condition for me; if we had twelve Novembers in a year I should write a work of genius.

All Souls' Day, All Saints' Day, Allhallow's Eve. Do you know what I wish? I wish that witches and goblins and leprechauns and Haunted Huntsmen and all such marvels were real. I wish that souls really did rise from the grave and dance on the headstones until cockcrow. I wish there were vampires, and djinns, and fairies living under toadstools. I want Baba Yaga to lie in her three-legged hut in the forest, and I want mermaids to swim in the grottoes of the sea, glimmering palely with their green hair floating behind them. Were there a Satan, I'd want him real, with horns and a forked tail, appearing in a puff of smoke and with a sulphurous smell. And real angels, with real wings and shining haloes! Oh, come back, all ye creatures of other words, half-worlds, underworlds, nether worlds—I'll take you back in trade. What'll I give? Why, bombs and other refinements of civilization: the electric chair, the gas chamber, and the automobile commercials on television.

"Hey, didja hear that? I 'most know how to whistle. I was doing that at kindergarten and Mrs. Allison heard me and she didn't know I knew how to whistle and I'm only four years old, isn't that *sneaky* of me to know how to whistle when I'm only four years old?"

The black cherry has lost almost all its leaves. The transparent apple has a few left, the dogwood has more, and the Japanese maple is a mass of red, yellow, orange, green, and brown. We haven't raked for a couple of days and the grass is littered with leaves. I don't mind; I like it that way. The corn is dry, still standing. A single nasturtium still blooms, out by the bean poles. In front there are marigolds and a few roses, and the tall white hydrangea is mummified, its flower petals still intact but dry as paper.

Duncan did something this morning I've been expecting him to do for a long time. He brushed his teeth with Brylcreem and put Colgate Toothpaste on his hair. (Unpaid adv't.)

When the mail comes in the morning, splatting down on the tile floor through the mail slot in the front door, I run for it with fingers crossed on both hands, saying, "Let it be something good!" I can tell an envelope from my agent upside down at ten paces, and I grab it with the ever-fresh hope that is a writer's necessary attitude toward the morning mail. But I don't open it—I open everything else first. I arrange the mail in reverse order, with circulars and bills on top, and then personal letters in order of increasing interest, and finally that tantalizing envelope from my agent. The circulars I drop into the trash. Sometimes I save the coupons worth 8 cents for about a week, and *then* I drop them in the trash. The bills I open and clip together and stuff into the proper corner of my desk drawer. By this time I am seething with impatience and I race through the personal letters so rapidly, with one eye on that long envelope at the bottom of the pile, that I always have to go back and read them all again.

But this morning it was worth it. I knew it the minute I slid the folded letter out of the envelope, because I could see there was only one sentence on the paper, and while I like chatty letters and am a tireless correspondent, the best letters from my agent always have one sentence or at the most two. This morning's sentence was, "Cosmopolitan is taking the story for $600—'Dream of the South Seas.' "

My wild whoop of delight nearly shattered the window-panes.

Cameron has at last made his birthday list. It begins with "an oil painting kit" (and he doesn't mean a paint-by-number set, thank goodness, but an honest set of tubes of paint, palette, brushes, turpentine, oil, scraper, and canvas paper) and continues with a list of about twenty Canadian postage stamps he wants, carefully noted down from the catalogue. And that is the total list. Urgings to augment it have produced nothing; he wants a new bicycle and a portable radio, but he knows he won't get either of them so he hasn't wasted any ink writing them down. This reminds me of the Christmas a couple of years ago when he grew so irritable and frustrated, trying to think of what he wanted, that he finally burst out in rage and despair, "I hate Christmas and I hope it never comes!" But at last it was Christmas Eve and the tree was up and I went up to tuck everybody in, and Cameron, with the end of tormented suspense at last in sight, with only sleep intervening now between him and Christmas morning, sighed deeply and pulled his blankets up to his chin. "Sugar plums will dance in my head tonight!" he said.

The doctor has me taking some marvelously tiny pills of a pale-purple hue, a color that reminds me of coats owned by old ladies riding on buses. They are supposed to slow me down. My hand is smeared with something that combines cortisone with chloromycetin. But—and the doctor agrees with me—the real trouble is in my head.

But who wants a frontal lobotomy for a case of *eczema?*

Scene: a dress shop. Enter MATRON juggling parcels.

CLERK: Oh, good morning! How are *you?*

MATRON: Fine. (Abstractedly) Fine, fine . . . what I want is a cocktail dress. Not too fancy . . . just . . . well, just a cocktail dress.

CLERK: What size?

MATRON: A fourteen or a sixteen. It depends.

CLERK: Here's a darling one . . .

MATRON: Not brown, please.

CLERK: This is lovely . . .

MATRON: No, I have a white one. I can't wear it, but I *have* it.

CLERK: This?

MATRON: Nooo . . . I can't wear that shade of blue. It makes my nose look red.

CLERK: (Trying not to look at MATRON's nose) Oh. Here's a beautiful one . . .

MATRON: (Obstinately) My husband can't stand fuchsia.

CLERK: Black, then. Here's a beautiful black, with shirring.

MATRON: I hadn't even considered black. And those cap sleeves—I don't know. It just doesn't . . . I'll try on that green one, with the jacket.

(CLERK and MATRON repair to fitting room. The green dress won't zip up the back and turns out to be a size thirteen. MATRON stands there disconsolate in her slip. Her feet hurt. This is the fourth shop she has been in.)

CLERK: Let me bring the black. I want to see how you look in it. (She sails out and comes back with the shirred black. It fits.) Come on out to the three-way mirror, please.

MATRON: (Viewing herself) I don't know. Black? Hmmm . . .

CLERK: Oh, Mr. Williams. Mr. Williams?

(MR. WILLIAMS, the store manager, pops out from behind a display.)

MR. WILLIAMS: Yes . . . Oh! Oh! Oh, my! My goodness!

CLERK: What size would you say this was, Mr. Williams?

(MATRON waits patiently; she knows what is coming but she waits to hear it anyway.)

MR. WILLIAMS: (Innocently) Why, a twelve?

CLERK: Mr. Williams, it's a *sixteen!*

MR. WILLIAMS: A sixteen! Why, I never would have . . . It certainly *looks* like a twelve. A *sixteen!*

CLERK: It's a copy of a Ceil Chapman, too. You can wear it *forever.*

MR. WILLIAMS: (Shaking his head in disbelief) A *sixteen* . . . !

(MATRON, knowing full well that CLERK and MR. WILLIAMS work together like Lunt and Fontanne, nevertheless buys the dress.)

An arctic front has moved over us and we shiver at only slightly below freezing, softies that we are. A thin dusting of powdery snow lay in the lee of the shingles on the garage roof this morning, just a little thicker than frost. Against the blue sky a few remaining leaves quiver on the dogwood; a good wind would dislodge them all. But the Japanese maple remains heavy with leaf, looking like a woman smugly wrapped in a red fox fur coat.

The story I padded so carefully for the CBC has been read over the air—drastically cut. There's no business like show business.

You may have perceived that we are not joiners. My college chapter of Phi Beta Kappa keeps sending me, tirelessly, all the proper notices of this and that, to which I never reply. I chose one P.T.A. out of the possible three to join this fall, but I am not a member in any real sense of the word; my joining is merely a monetary contribution, like "joining" the Red Cross when you put your dime in the second-grade collection box, and I go to meetings only when the topic interests me. The university faculty wives' club has given me up—I have refused to Keep Fit with them or to participate in Flower Arrangement, Current Events, Play Reading, or anything else. I am a lousy faculty wife and it is a good thing I don't seriously believe that a woman who can wear a hat and pour tea is an asset to a professor's career or I would be worried about my husband's future.

Our social life, moreover, is restricted to having friends over in ones, twos, and threes, occasionally filling the house with students, and attending other people's parties. A dinner party would throw me into a panic, anyway, and besides, we have no dining room, no dining table, and only four good dinner plates, so the possibilities are somewhat limited.

The truth is that with six children we don't feel the need of a social life in a general way. What we really need is more in the nature of an *anti*social life.

I am tired of hearing people sing "Ol' Man River" with the words "Darkies all work on the Mississippi" replaced by "Here we all work . . ." This seems as silly as objecting to books in which white rabbits marry black rabbits. I wonder if the people who fight to have *Little Black Sambo* removed from children's libraries don't really feel, deep down inside, that to be black is intrinsically unfortunate?

Little Black Sambo is a lovely book and who can fail to love its hero? Where does the book imply that there is anything at all wrong with being black? Zealots, search your souls: I think some of you think that if we don't *say* anything or use the words that identify a Negro as a Negro, the problem will vanish. The real problem is to be able to say Negro or even black without anybody reacting unfavorably.

A bamboo rake leans accusingly against the trunk of the apple tree, but with the temperature standing at 30° I'm not going outside to use it. When it gets this cold here we all act as if it were 30 *below;* I don't know what would happen to us if we ever had to move to a place where temperatures actually drop radically in the winter. I hate things such as gloves and fur-lined boots and woolen scarves, and the idea of wearing the kind of underwear known as "snuggies" (ugh) fills me with horror. I don't even like to tie a kerchief over my head in the rain. Maybe I am really a nudist at heart?

We still haven't (1) painted the new cement floor in the basement, which generates a nice, fine dust when it's walked on, (2) got that new fence we need, (3) done anything about our overcrowded, doubled-up books, our leaky eavestrough, our grisly pink bathroom downstairs and our jaundiced-pachyderm bathroom upstairs and the tub with lion-paw feet and curling linoleum underneath. And there is also the driveway that ought to be blacktopped, the basement walls that should be sealed with wallboard, the bedroom floors that ought to be repainted or sanded or something, the kitchen wallpaper with those bilious fruits on it, and the stair carpet worn through at every tread. If I make money will I do interesting things like driving a sports car with my bare feet at 90 mph and cracking up? No, I will buy new sheets and blankets and have the driveway blacktopped.

And what's more, my new washing machine has been out of order for the better part of a week. I went downstairs to get the nice clean spun-dry laundry out to toss into the drier and instead I found the machine full of dirty blue-black water and jeans sloshing away disconsolately long after the timer had moved around through the full cycle to OFF. With imprecations and cries of rage and despair, I fished out the jeans, dumping liberal amounts of water into my loafers, and spent a futile half hour on the phone trying to lure a repairman out here. Nothing doing until Friday, and now, after days of doing laundry by hand in the sink (we never have enough clothes to last more than two days), Friday has arrived, and here I sit—waiting.

Why hasn't anyone invented a laborsaving gadget to save the housewife the labor of sitting around waiting for some fool man to show up and repair some fool laborsaving gadget?

Cameron has finished his first oil painting—Chianti bottle, two apples, two bananas. For a ten-year-old, it is a very interesting primitive. Andy has been doing some work in oils, using the ancient palette, brushes, and paraphernalia from my Art Students' League days, but he was content to leave his paints up in his room and leave his paintings rolled up or tacked rather hastily to his bedroom wall. He also left his palette on a chair so that he sat on it, creating a lovely Jackson Pollock on the seat of a pair of gray jeans. Cameron, on the other hand, has gone to work and cleaned out a corner of the basement, set up the easel, stenciled two signs saying ART GALLERY, and has hung half a dozen of Andy's canvases as well as his own. Cameron is a perfectionist.

Winter, unexpected and a month early, has arrived. We awoke to see white rooftops, and this precipitated a wild rush to the dime store for mittens and to the local bootery for boots. The first snowmen of the season, rather dirty because the snow was so thin that a lot of dirt got rolled up with it, are standing outside with carrot noses. Boots stand in puddles in the hall, while mittens lie on the furnace registers or stick up from the backs of kitchen chairs in expressions of shock and dismay. Wet parkas and snowsuits hang on the doorknobs. In the living room a fire burns and the children sit cozily by the television, eating a huge bowl of popcorn, and I, alone in the kitchen nook, have been eating a small bowl and reading the *Saturday Review* to the accompaniment of a concert on the radio. Wayne is out, despite the snow, attending an evening lecture.

I wouldn't mind winter at all, not the snow nor the cold, if only someone would give me (1) a place to put wet boots, (2) some kind of little tree on which to hang six pairs of mittens to dry, and (3) an automatic snowsuit-shucking machine for small children.

Polly began watching *Fidelio* on television yesterday and wept and howled when she had to leave it for ten minutes to bolt her supper. She sat totally absorbed for the entire production, breaking her silence with but one puzzled question. Rocco, the jailer, and Fidelio were in the dungeon, digging the grave for Florestan, who sat despondent in his chains, bearded and tattered. Polly watched, a curious and intent look on her face, and finally she could bear her problem no longer: "But, Mommy!"

she cried. "I thought people were always buried *in their best clothes!*"

Jill also watched, and she also had a question. "Does that girl *want* to be boy?" she asked, incredulously. We explained. "Maybe if we watch tomorrow," Jill said at last, "she'll go home and put on a *dress*."

Malcolm has been spoiling to indulge his passion for taxidermy and has felt a little put out that we did not consider our *Rattus rattus rattus* a fit subject for stuffing. No dead birds have turned up in the yard, and just where he is to find a small dead animal I don't know. Malcolm is a rural child misplaced in an urban setting, and yesterday he just couldn't bear it any longer, so he became a sort of taxidermist-in-reverse. He took down the pink-antlered deer head from the front porch and *un*stuffed it, ending up with antlers and a skull, the basement floor covered with excelsior, and a hunk of rather mangy hide of no conceivable use to anyone. It was an awful mess but he was in seventh heaven while making it.

"Mom," says Jill, "if you have a dog and a cat and a whole bunch of kids, that will be fair because then you won't be lonely."

What does she mean, *if?*

Are there any *good* things about being a writer? Why, yes, there's this morning, when I put on my coat to go shopping and just as I got to the front door the postman dropped an envelope in at my feet—an unexpected check for German rights to a very old story of mine. I took it right along to the bank, cashed it and promptly spent every penny of it and more, on four bathrobes for the boys and a new sweater for Duncan.

I have the rather bad habit of measuring my literary success by cash alone. Well, I like earning money because I like being able to spend it. But even if I were fabulously wealthy, I am constantly astonished at the vast number of things I simply don't want. I don't want:

(1) a mink coat or any kind of fur
(2) diamonds or any kind of real jewels
(3) more than five pairs of shoes at once
(4) a yacht
(5) a new hat (I don't even want my *old* hats)
(6) an electric coffee pot, an electric mixer, an electric blender, an electric hot-dog cooker, an electric blanket
(7) 97 per cent of everything I see when I go shopping, especially pottery figurines, black ceramic panthers, wall plaques and all kinds of cute salt-and-pepper shakers, cute cooky jars, cute everything.

Alas, alas, for the children at least, the snow has gone and the temperature has risen back to the mid-forties. Duncan has come home from the library with books by Zilboorg, Menninger, and Morris Cohen, having just polished off Fred Hoyle on the nature of the universe. Mac, on the other hand, has just come home from the drugstore with a bottle of stuff to put on his fingernails so he will stop nibbling at them. Is this part of the new Malcolm, *interested in girls?*

Duncan, puzzled over the Lady Chatterly fuss, wants to know why four-letter words are four-letter words and why there is no hope of restoring them to ordinary use to describe in an ordinary way the functions they describe. "After all," he says, "from the standpoint of the species, sex is the most important function we perform, so why should there be a dirty word for it?" And we go on to imagine a society of intelligent amoeboid creatures for whom binary fission has some equivalent, unrepeatable, four-letter word; the absurdity of it is illuminating.

Can you imagine some low-minded amoeba writing REND on a lavatory wall?

Mac insists he wants a small dead animal for his birthday.

I have forgotten all about dieting. The trouble is that nobody nags me and I don't have time to nag myself. I'm not fat and I'm not getting any fatter, but I'm not getting any thinner either; that same old ten pounds lingers on. I have been trying to remember where it was I read the vital statistics of the Venus de Milo, because it seemed to me that mine were astonishingly similar. That *ought* to reassure me, but if you try to imagine the Venus de Milo in a pair of pedal pushers you can see why it doesn't reassure me very much.

I can't wander around just clutching a bit of slipping drapery. Not in November anyway.

Wayne has promised a colleague he'll go to the bullfights with him in Mexico City. I can't help recalling that he once became dizzy and nearly fainted during a physiology lecture on the circulation of the blood. Hmm.

The children have submitted their Christmas lists:

DUNCAN: physics kit
brainiac computer
old clock
go to an auction
interesting electronic apperratus
tools—file, vise, tapered reamer, electric drill

ANDY: modle plane for gas engine size 15 to 29 (no engine)
mystries

MAC: jazz—Louis Armstrong
Strauss Waltzes
Max books
stamp hinges
stamp tongs
cashbox with lock
bisecting kit
microscope
(and a long, long list of U.S. postage stamps)

CAM: castle with knights and outlaws
battery-operated phone set
puppet theater

And POLLY (writing for both herself and Jill):
a doll carrig
a fridg and stov
buzy bees
a pianno
a woodin truk
unbrelas
little anamuls
teddy bear
Yogi bear
Ragedy Andy
Puzls

I've already looked at the physics kit in question at the top of Duncan's list and have vetoed it as outrageously expensive; Cam's list is the end result of a desperate search through a Sears catalogue, and he doesn't really want any of it very much. The truth is that the boys are outgrowing Christmas just a little; every year it is harder for them to think of what they want. It isn't that they don't want a lot of things—they do, all year round; but at Christmas when the possibility of getting what they ask for is close and immediate, making choices and composing a list are tasks almost beyond their emotional endurance. Suppose, on December 26, one of them should suddenly think of that one wonderful thing he *really* wanted! I think such a frightening event is always in their heads and the sugar plums have a pretty cramped place in which to dance.

Why do heathens like us celebrate Christmas? I don't know. And Christmas carols make me cry.

November is about to vanish and I hate to see it go. The lawn is littered with soggy dark-brown leaves and even the Japanese maple is nearly nude. The corn patch seems to be full of crumpled ghosts, and the wind has blown down another section of fence. Today is foggy but a little sun is striking through and hitting the dogwood branches. I hear a foghorn, miles away. Virginia has been here unexpectedly for supper. She looked so much the same that I felt for a moment that I had only dreamed the marriage and the baby; but Wayne drove her home to the Indian reserve with a huge box of baby things, a plastic inflatable baby bathtub which used to be Cameron's and must therefore be ten years old, a pink bunting, and a diaper pail. Superstitiously, having given away all our baby things, I cross my fingers to ward off pregnancy. We have begun our Christmas shopping and I wait for a school morning and then sneak out the LP of Louis Armstrong and play it for myself. I wash and iron and fold and pack Wayne's shirts and off he goes to the airport, bound for Chicago. I discover the one (and only) compensation for his absence: I can leave my typewriter here in the kitchen nook and eat in the midst of heaps of paper and x'd-out first drafts of things. I go through the budget and find that, while $70 vanished last month, $87 appeared from nowhere this month. I am simply going to accept it gracefully and not ask too many questions.

Speaking of questions:

Mom, what kind of salmon brings the highest price on the market?

Mom, is this right?

Mom, how do you factor this equation?

Mom, are salmon caught in fresh water in nets or in salt water in nets?

Mom, look, if x squared plus 8x plus 12 . . .

(I had algebra twenty-two years ago and haven't used it since. I make a feeble protest.)

You're not interested in my work, that's what!

What's the abbreviation for Oregon, Mom?

Where's the ruler?

Would you check these over, Mom?

Hey, Mom, I figured it out, want me to show you? It's real neat. See, if you have x squared plus 6x, then you have x plus 3 times x plus three plus 9 equals . . .

Do you have to do that out loud, hey?

I crawled through a broken window into a vacant house. I crawled through a broken window into a vacant house. I crawled through . . .

Mom. Mom! What's Cam *doing?*

(I don't know. Cam, what are you doing?)

Memorizing. I have to tell a story out loud. I crawled through a broken window into a vacant house. I crawled . . .

Mom, can I have some scotch tape?

Let's see, x squared . . .
I crawled through a broken window . . .

A postcard arrives airmail from Wayne. A scenic view of Chicago? Oh no, three heads: Java man, Neanderthal man, Cro-Magnon man, from the Field Museum. Other mail and children's drawings and pieces of schoolwork start piling up on his worktable in the study. He will be home Sunday morning. I count, squinting out the window into the late afternoon sky, and ascertain that there are precisely four leaves left on the dogwood tree.

I love bare trees against the sky.

DECEMBER

DECEMBER is, first of all, no month in which to attempt to finish a book. It may seem a tidy idea to start a book in January and wind it up in December, mailing it off with the last of the Christmas cards (on about January 2), but I know from experience that planning to do anything in December other than merely survive is expecting too much. It is even foolhardy to expect to finish one's Christmas shopping in December.

December is not exactly my favorite month. We have managed, through some execrably bad planning, to cram two birthdays into the month, one of them a mere four days before Christmas. There's an argument for Planned Parenthood for you: who in his right mind would want to be born right before Christmas? In fact, I've considered suggesting to the Planned Parenthood people that they designate late November and early December as Official Planned Breeding Season, so that five-year-olds all across the nation would turn six when school opens in the fall, thus removing from the necks of principals and school boards the burden of deciding which five-and-a-half-year-olds get in and which five-and-a-half-year-olds stay out. If we're going to plan these things we might as well plan them *thoroughly*.

In addition to the birthdays, December has school holidays, the children are at home, it rains, and Wayne is up to his eyebrows in exams, muttering and fuming and occasionally breaking out into a short laugh that has as much despair in it as humor. Add to all this the nasty habit the American Anthropological Association has of scheduling its annual meetings between Christmas and New Year's, and you have Wayne not only grading papers but also writing a paper to deliver at the meetings. Christmas funds are depleted by travel costs, and my Christmas cheer is depleted by the thought of being left alone to cope with the cluttered, tinsel-strewn, child-infested house during the so-called holidays. There will be one child who will break his favorite gift on December 26; there will be one who will sit down and calculate what we must have spent on each item, and he will discover that he has been gypped; and there will be a child who, although he got nearly everything he asked for, didn't get anything "to *do*," and he will wander about disconsolately, playing with one of Jill's toys until he succeeds in breaking it.

December brings the hope of snow, but a vain hope and rarely satisfied. Nevertheless, December is tinsel and holly and candles and nuts and stars and candy canes and Salvation Army kettles at the door of the dime store. It's the smell of Douglas fir and the taste of postal glue. It's the constant cry of the Red-eyed Common Wrapper to her mate, "Where's the scotch tape?"

And it's lists, lists, lists, mostly composed of people's names, each one followed by an obstinate and unanswerable question mark. Television commercials in which people obliterate these miserable ?'s by giving everybody a gift carton of cigarettes are of no use to us. We know more nonsmokers than the American Tobacco Company would admit the existence of.

It is December 1. All the leaves that intend to fall have now fallen. I meant to do so much today but here I am, with student manuscripts still to plow through, the living-room windows still to clean, and all I've done is wash my hair. Last night, actually, was when I intended to do the manuscripts, but I got started making a hand puppet out of one of Wayne's old socks, so instead of winding up the evening with a pile of marked papers and typed criticisms I wound up with a nice dark-gray creature with black ears edged in pink blanket stitching, a blue nose, and long, pale-blue eyelashes above yellow button eyes. He's a Gnu and his name is Gnigel, and I think he ought to talk with a retired British colonel voice and appear on television along with Flanders and Swann and Shari Lewis. However, he has his domestic uses; Jill didn't want to get up this morning, but I took Gnigel upstairs and *he* asked her to get up, and she did.

The first signs of Christmas are in the house: packages piling up to be mailed, a small table covered with wrappings and ribbons in the bedroom, and two large gold star bursts hanging from the beam in the living room. But I still haven't taken the snapshot of the children for our

Christmas card picture and any day now the first card will arrive in the mail. It happens every year.

The first card, however, is never really *from* anybody. It's always from a real-estate company, or British-American Oil, or the Bank of Montreal.

Wayne reads me the reviews of *Ben-Hur* while I am eating and reading something else—this being a bad habit we share and indulge each other in mutually.

"*You* can take the boys," I say without looking up. I like nice small movies with about six people in the cast.

Which reminds me, somehow, that our druggist insists on calling me, facetiously, "Mrs. Metalious"—which causes some sudden stares. But I, more's the financial pity of it, could never have written *Peyton Place.* I'm just not interested. I find the cerebrations of Timofey Pnin in Nabokov's *Pnin* or of Alexandre Chenevert in Gabrielle Roy's *The Cashier* much more to my taste than the feverish thoughts of some female caressing the welts on her thighs. Pile horror upon horror and perversion upon perversion and I turn off my emotions and read with all the involvement of an IBM computer. I read *Peyton Place* without once being moved about anybody in it, while *The Cashier* had me laughing, weeping, exclaiming, and delighting page by page.

I am dreaming again of what I shall write next year. I have been told by an authority on such matters that a character I have been thinking about is impossible and will never be taken to the public's heart. And why? Because he has a partial plate. I am dumfounded. Certainly the world must be full of men with partial plates who are nevertheless dearly loved. All you women who love men who have partial plates, you must rise to my defense.

All you dental technicians, too.

Jill informs me that her friend Sandy's mother has also made a puppet, just like mine. I have a niggling doubt in my mind. "What's *it's* name?" I ask.

"Oh . . . Gnigel," she answers, airily.

"Now that we know his name is Gnigel," says Malcolm, *sotto voce*, "we know Sandy's mother didn't make any puppet."

Polly, trying to reach an unreachable itch the other day, expressed a desire to own a Chinese backscratcher. "Oh, no!" Jill cried. "Why, they're dangerous! Why, I saw a woman buy one of those downtown and when she scratched her back it went right through to the other side and the blood all came out and she *died*. You don't want one of *those!*"

Four and a half is an *interesting* age.

It is pouring rain, dampening my intentions of going Christmas shopping this afternoon after the children come home. You couldn't pay me to go out in this stuff. But the dogwood branches are festooned with lovely, shining tears; I sit and watch, waiting for one to gather enough weight to fall.

A less lovely item is the dustmop head, hanging on the clothesline.

The sodden garden looks utterly, thoroughly, irrevocably dead.

This house is in its usual condition. Gnigel the Gnu is lying on the windowsill next to a coffee cup full of dregs. On the same windowsill are: my little vial of purple pills, a sugar bowl, a Breck Shampoo carton full of seashells from San Juan Island, two buttons, *Doctor Zhivago* (untouched), Theodora Kroeber's *The Inland Whale* (a lovely book), three badges to sew on Cameron's uniform sleeve, two letters to be mailed, my calorie counter (tsk-tsk), a pencil, and dust. On the chair nearest me are an empty Japanese orange crate, a hula hoop, the jacket to Jill's plaid dress, the newest Sunday *New York Times*, and a straw hat from Ensenada.

House Beautiful should send out somebody to take pictures. It would make women feel better all across the continent.

Why is it that boys who have grunted at you all afternoon, moaned and groaned over homework half the evening, fought and kicked among themselves, been uncivil and more or less loathsome up through nine and ten o'clock, suddenly become, at scant minutes to eleven, civilized, intelligent, interesting conversationalists? We progressed last night from a discussion of the emigrations of lemmings to the problem of the whooping crane, through a brief introduction to the work of Muir, Burroughs, and Audubon, a scurry to the encyclopedia to find out about the passenger pigeon, and a sad commentary on the near-disappearance of the buffalo, to (with an inexplicable shift) the poetry of Coleridge, Homer, Milton, and Dante.

Our first Christmas card has arrived—from the public relations officer of the Salvation Army.

"Mommy, did Mary go to the Safeway?" "Mary? What do you mean, did Mary go to the Safeway?" (We don't know any Mary.)

"I mean, Mommy, well, where did Mary get her food, Mommy? For her and the baby Jesus?"

The clouds are weeping inconsolably over some heavenly sorrow and the temperature stands at 45° out on the back porch, this being for us a very usual dead-of-winter temperature. Prairie folk who come here to retire have a tough time scraping up a bit of Yuletide spirit in the face of this climate of ours. But Jill is engaged in rapidly increasing the Christmas spirit inside the house with the various bits of decoration that she brings home from kindergarten. Today it was some bare branches in an orange-juice can, each tiny twig hung with a painted "flower" cut from the shaped bottoms of egg cartons and sprinkled with glitter. Malcolm suggests that her teacher probably stays up all night manufacturing these things for the children to take home so that the parents will marvel at what a good kindergarten it is. How cynical can you get?

"Mommy . . . when *my* mother makes cookies, she gives me a little bit of dough to make my own cooky out of."

"Oh, does she?"

"And when I have my cooky all made, she says . . . *my* mother does . . . she says, Oh goodness, what a lovely cooky you have made for a little girl only four years old."

"She must be a nice mommy."

"Oh, she's a very nice mommy. She always lets me do that."

"What does your mommy look like?"

"Well, *my* mother . . . she has black pants like yours and a shirt like yours and hair like yours, and she's wearing her black pants and her shirt right now. And she's making cookies, too."

"Do you suppose it would be all right if I gave you a little bit of dough to make your own cooky, like your mother does?"

"Um-hum! . . . Mommy, *my* mother has the same name as your name, too."

The Christmas card snapshot has at last been taken. Mindful of previous years in which efforts to get all six lined up and smiling at once resulted only in hysterics, I resorted to standing behind the television set while they sat mesmerized by an ancient Popeye cartoon. I have just seen the results, brought up dripping from the basement by Duncan; such earnest, sober faces! They look at if they were watching *On the Beach*, instead.

I haven't finished the shopping. I haven't made a fruitcake, and I won't either. But I *have* been to the Christmas concert, I *have* frosted the cookies for the tree and sprinkled them with those tooth-shattering gold and silver balls, I *have* remembered to buy silver rain for the tree, I *have* been to the doctor to show him my almost-well eczematous hand, and I *have* given my last lecture until after the holidays. Cheers, cheers!

No school Christmas concert is complete without one child who makes some terrible mistake, misses his cue, forgets his lines, or can't get on or off the stage properly. This is an essential part of the entertainment; if a concert went off perfectly and without incident, I think the audience would go home feeling vaguely disturbed. Last night it was a sweet little girl in a yellow dress. She stood at stage right with two little companions, and three other little children—all of them first-graders—stood at stage left. Below them, in the pit as it were, sang the carolers: "We wish you a Merry Christmas, We wish you a Merry Christmas, We wish you a Merry Christmas and a Happy New Year!"

Down bent the three on stage left and up they came with three printed cards to hold up. Down bent two on stage right and up again with one long card to hold up. But our little girl in the yellow dress, entranced by the sea of parental faces, moved not at all. The printed message read—CHRISTMAS . . . HAPPY NEW YEAR. The little girl clutching CHRISTMAS joggled her arm, pointing down at forgotten MERRY at her feet. She burst into tears, she shook her head vigorously, she refused to pick it up at all. The carol ended, the carolers turned to leave, and the six on stage were to exit at stage left. The little girl was the last to go; she got to the middle of the stage, realized that MERRY was still lying on the floor, cried even harder, ran back and picked it up, and finally got across that vast empty stage and made her exit—to the loudest applause of the evening.

This was not applause born of pity or sympathy. This was pure appreciation. She had supplied that certain something.

How dear to my heart are the scenes of my childhood . . .

Well, every once in a while, as in every household populated by people and not mechanical dolls, *we* have a Scene.

Cameron is a shrieker. We have tried to tell him the story of the Little Boy Who Cried Wolf, but it makes no impression on him; at the slightest imposition or physical aggression, no matter how infinitesimal, Cameron shrieks. We have hardened ourselves to this as much as we can, and someday Cameron will get caught in the maw of an infernal machine, or will find himself hanging precariously over an abyss, or will be menaced by a brace of tigers or a pack of eight-foot Abominable Snowmen, and he will shriek and shriek and shriek, and we won't pay any mind.

Last night he began shrieking at the dinner table.

Absolutely nothing much was going on, but he was shrieking nevertheless, at some fancied injury or other. We managed to survive the meal and ship the children out of the kitchen—where we all eat—into the living room, so that we could sit peacefully for a moment or two collecting our senses and exchanging a rare uninterrupted sentence. From the living room the shrieking continued, signifying nothing; but then Malcolm, for some reason or other, began to imitate it, and Mac's imitations are always ten times as loud and ten times as maddening as the originals. I rose from my chair, caught Mac by the arm, and dragged him into the bathroom, where I got a roll of adhesive tape and proceeded to snip off a generous portion, back Malcolm into a corner, and plaster his mouth shut. By this time both he and I were giggling, but this important development was lost on Polly and Jill, who fancied that I was about to do Mac some dreadful injury and descended on me with pummeling fists in Mac's defense, screaming rage and vengeance. It was magnificent—such sibling unity! No, when the chips are down, no matter how much the children may quarrel among themselves, all the children are together, solid, indivisible, antiparental, all for one and one for all. Even as I winced under the hail of blows and tried to explain that Mac was laughing and not crying, I felt proud of their fearless attack.

Most of our Scenes involve Malcolm, who works hard at living up to the stereotype of the inflammable redhead. It was Mac who smashed the window and got glass into the *Boeuf à la Flamande,* Mac who in the least personal crisis threatens murder, mayhem, and suicide ("I'll jump off the roof!"). But it is also Mac who finds thermometers, borrows rubbing alcohol, remembers where things are, manages the smaller children best, and often seems to know what needs to be done long before he is asked to do it. And it is also Mac who bites his nails, loves music, hates haircuts, screams at me at least twelve times a week that I'm *not fair,* and is the most fun to take along on a shopping trip or to a museum.

Any parent who says he loves all his children equally and alike has managed some kind of triumph of mechanical intellect over the human heart or else is not telling the truth. I know, at least, that any six children as unalike as ours are bound to inspire different kinds of love, equal in quantity perhaps, but different in texture. Duncan we love with pride mixed with exasperation, Malcolm we love with a pang at his frustrations and furies. Andy we love with quiet pleasure and still a hint of anxiety, for the very reasonableness that makes him so easy to get along with also makes him at times withdrawn and remote. Cameron, even while he is shrieking, we love with a fond smile and a suspension of criticism; he is less demanding of us and I suppose we are less demanding of him. Polly we love with a bit of wonder and our breath held; will that promise of blonde, green-eyed, golden-skinned beauty be fulfilled, and will she ever get out of that sulky, sassy stage? Jill we love with a hug and a kiss and a Band-Aid on the knee—and a slippery, desperate grasp on the reins, trying to keep her wild, exuberant, overflowing ego in check.

I have been pressed into service as a script typist. It seems that the children of Cameron's grade are going to have a party on Friday, the last day before the holidays, and each child must contribute something to the entertainment. Cam and three of his friends have decided to put on a play, and Cam—the ringleader—has chosen to stage a repeat performance of the summer's success, "The

Creation of Frankenstein's Monster." Here is the script, laboriously printed out at the kitchen table before dinner:

> The Doctor asks Zarcoff to get Carloff. He brings him back and the Docter tells them he is going to make a human. He tells them to fetch surtain things as kidnees, lungs, and such. Then he tells Carloff to go to the museum and fetch a brain and the Docter said to get the smart one and NOT the dum one and don't break it.
>
> Carloff was a pretty dum guy so he brought back the right one but it was broken. The Docter said, "YOU FOOL IT'S BROKEN GET OUT!!"
>
> Zarcoff and the Doc. are talking and saying, "Since that Carloff is so Dum and we haven't got a brain for the human We'll kill him and get his, so as soon as he comes back in you get him." After he had killed him they put in the brain and said, "Now all we need is blood." Then Zarcoff said we'll get it from Carloff, the Doc said, "Yah, that's what I was thinking so they syfuned the blood from Carloff to the man made human. For the finishing thing we need the blood curculating, Zarcoff go get the pump. So he got the pump and they got the blood curculating. After they had finished they stoped a moment and Zarcoff said Look out it's a monster it's coming strait for us! Doc look out!
>
> The montser killed the Doc, and Zarcoff went up to the Doc and looked at him. Then the monster came and killed Zarcoff.

No one could possibly convince Cameron that this might be a little unsuitable for the fifth grade; but never mind, even the teacher okayed the idea. Why am I to raise a dissenting voice?

The month is more than half over and Christmas is rushing closer; I can feel its hot breath on my neck. I have been gluing snapshots on notepaper and manufacturing our Christmas cards; packages are piling up in our bedroom and an invitation to a New Year's Eve party is tacked rather forlornly—already regretfully declined—on the bulletin board, where I shall glance at it at midnight, December 31, and curse the American Anthropological Association while Wayne sees the New Year come in down in Mexico City. (Oh, well, there is nothing more ridiculous than a bunch of college professors standing around blowing horns and wearing silly hats and trying to look gay and abandoned when the clock strikes twelve.) Cameron has been making decorations out of construction paper, and Jill draws one Christmas angel after another, wonderfully gay and lighthearted little angels with wide smiles, gold crayoned wings, shining haloes—and red hair. The kindergarten has had its Christmas party, such an exciting affair, Jill reports, that one little boy couldn't quite bear the tension; he threw up. Wayne is still grading Anthropology 200 exams and writing his paper, but we sneak an afternoon now and then to hunt frantically for things on our list. It's amazing how many antique and secondhand stores don't have an old clock that won't run. All the old clocks in town seem to be running fine; but what Duncan wants is one that isn't running, so he can fix it. Maybe we shall end up buying one that runs, and breaking it, although somehow or other that doesn't appeal to me. What do you do with children who want dead animals and broken clocks, anyway?

Mac has gone through the elbows of his one good school shirt again.

Add to the confusion: Duncan borrowing the neighbors' electric handsaw (there's a noise I can't abide), Polly trying to finish a dish towel she is embroidering for a Christmas gift, Cam mounting one of his oil paintings, Andy getting ready for a party, Mac playing the guitar, Jill skipping rope in the front hall, and me trying to make a chocolate mousse for dinner. The Christmas cards are flooding in and only trickling out. And Andy just went through the elbows of *his* good school shirt.

Wayne whipped off to the campus yesterday with his paper for the departmental secretary to type and whipped right back and handed it to *me*, two other guys having got there fustest with the mostest. So I spent last night typing his paper.

We have located an old wall clock with a pendulum—and it *doesn't* work!

Christmas is over and it is the evening of Boxing Day, December 26, and Wayne is high in the air somewhere, on his way to Mexico City. I have kept my envy nicely in check, but right now I would settle for eleven days even in Scranton, Pennsylvania.

Shall I write a lyrical page about Christmas? Shall I write of the togetherness of putting up the tree and singing carols afterwards (and leave out the furious argument about what color light to put inside the star, and Jill's screaming because she didn't know all the words)? Shall I write of how we woke in the morning before it grew light, and tiptoed upstairs and called the children down to the tree, glowing in the dark living room (and leave out the long sleepless night during which Duncan got up and tramped around upstairs every time the mantel clock struck the hour and the half hour)? Shall I write of the shining eyes and cries of delight (and leave out Cameron's howls of rage as he tried to decipher the directions for putting together his medieval castle, and Mac's fit of frustration when there was dust on his microscope lens and no lens paper to clean it with)? Shall I write of the Christmas dinner roasting in the oven (and leave out the temporary dysfunction of the oven thermocouple, and my dancing around the kitchen in desperation and anxiety, eying the clock and the cold, uncooked meal while Duncan took the top off the stove and tinkered with it and littered the floor with burnt matches)? Shall I write of the joys of Christmas toys (and leave out the fact that Jill has already gone back to playing with an old, gray, nasty piece of Silly Putty about three months old)?

Oh, let's not be *too* honest, shall we?

The year is running out—an ordinary year, a year in which nothing has happened, at least nothing much. Next year—or the year after, anyway—we must all ride bicycles around the world, or become pioneers at the headwaters of the Amazon, or go teach madrigals to the pygmies in the Congo, or scuba-dive off Wrangell Island. Now there would be a book!

Look who's talking. I can't even get up enough energy to go shopping for dinner; I've been prowling the cupboards trying to concoct imaginary dinners out of what's there. I have nine eggs, a jar of Manischewitz borscht that nobody likes but me, a piece of Roquefort, some stale bread, a pint of sour cream, two tomatoes . . . (Somewhere in Mexico City Wayne is eating tacos and enchiladas and drinking Mexican beer.) There aren't even any candy canes or cookies left on the tree. I do have a bottle of gin, which will do nicely for me but it doesn't seem suitable for the children.

And yet, even with nothing happening, so much remains unsaid. I guess I like this ordinary life; there are things about it I wouldn't trade for the excitement and glamour of a lot of extraordinary lives. I'm my own boss. I can run my house any way I want to. I can have a cup of coffee or a cup of tea without waiting for the hands of the clock to point to a sacred coffee break. I can fill the house with music of my own choosing, sometimes even of my own rather off-key making. No one watches me; I can dance with the broom and talk to the dishwater. I don't have to pick my lunch from a menu at a counter, or pack it in a paper bag; I open the refrigerator and pounce on a cold slice of last night's liver, or the remains of a carton of cottage cheese. I can darn socks and clean out the sewing basket and feel virtuous, or build a fire in the fireplace and watch an old movie on television and feel sinful.

Certainly there are dozens of things about myself, the children, the house which I would like to change if I had a magic wand. *Ping!* I would make us all sweet-tempered. *Ping!* I would double our income. *Ping!* I would have a new stair carpet, a repainted kitchen, a big refrigerator with room for twelve eggs, all of Beethoven's symphonies on LP's, a black-topped driveway, a clean house. *Ping!* Mac would no longer bite his nails, Duncan would comb his hair out of his eyes, Cameron would stop shrieking. *Ping!* Wayne would type his own papers and stop hoarding bills from the bookstore and the Faculty Club until they're two months overdue. *Ping!* I would already have written The Book I Am Supposed to Be Writing.

But if I am ambitious and dissatisfied, I am also full of daily, eternal, enduring pleasure. I am, I think, the happiest malcontent I know.

I am sitting here in the littered kitchen nook, looking out into the gray winter afternoon. The trees are black, the grass sodden and dispirited. *Doctor Zhivago* still sits on the windowsill, untouched. Tinsel is creeping through the house—I found some upstairs yesterday—and the kitchen faucet is dripping. (*Ping!* A new faucet!) I've been forgetting to take my little purple pills, but my hand is almost all well now. I'm getting a head cold instead. A week from today I start teaching again, the old two-nights-a-week routine once more; but the darkest day of the year is past and now it grows lighter day by day and before you know it I'll be out hunting for the first snowdrops under the rhododendron bushes by the front steps.

Do you know something? I never did make new curtains for the girls' bedroom, nor get a new typewriter, nor get my desk drawer repaired. But I must remember to count my blessings. At the delicatessen the other day I overheard a poor woman telling a friend that her gardener had been out covering the swimming pool and had come in to report to her that it had *sprung a leak*. You can't tell what real troubles people have until you get out among them and see how they live. All I could do was just shake my head and be grateful we don't have a swimming pool.

I look at the calendar and I can't really believe it. Why, Malcolm is already working up his February case of sinusitis! Why, in less than three months I'll be thirty-eight, and what have I got to show for it—six noisy kids, a husband with a beard, a run-down house, a pile of old tattered magazines full of stories about pregnant women, and ten extra pounds. Tomorrow morning I will get up at eight o'clock, have a cup of coffee and start making *lists.* And then I shall clean up the house, and do the laundry, and make the lunch, and write out checks for all the bills that fall due on January first. I could stop and meditate soberly on the Meaning of Life, but I don't think I will. More likely I'll go around the house, looking at the faded curtains and the ragged stair carpet and the linoleum under the bathtub, and try to arrange things in some kind of irrational, emotional priority. By evening I'll be exhausted just thinking about all the things I have to do next year. I'll sit in the kitchen nook and stare into space, listening to the clock ticking, and take a fresh sheet of paper and start to write down my New Year's Resolutions:

(1) Write another book
(2) Lose ten pounds . . .